Women in Film Noir

edited by E. Ann Kaplan

BFI Publishing

791. 436 ~~~~~~352 KAP
80743

Published by the
British Film Institute
21 Stephen Street, London W1P 1PL

Typesetting by Dark Moon
Printed by Garden House Press Ltd., Perivale, Middlesex
Cover by John Gibbs

First edition 1978
Revised edition 1980
Reprinted 1981, 1984, 1987, 1989, 1992, 1994

ISBN 0 85170 105 1

Contents

Acknowledgements

Stills are courtesy of Alex Gottlieb Productions, Allied Artists, British Film Institute, Columbia, F.D.A., International Pictures, King Bros., M.G.M., Paramount, Rank, Republic, RKO Radio, Twentieth Century Fox, Warner Bros. Special thanks to the Stills Department of the British Film Institute.

For Brett

Introduction

Looking at the place of women in film noir means the study of an essential aspect of this group of films, and constitutes a useful contribution, as evidenced by the essays here, to our understanding of the placing of women within cultural production. The BFI Summer School in 1975, which I attended, had been concerned with the area of film noir as genre, and the idea for this project resulted from that work and from a paper by Sylvia Harvey (revised for this monograph).

One of the depressing aspects of the study of women in art works is the repetition of the same structures, showing the strong hold of patriarchy. The cinema is no exception and in her two-part essay on *Klute*, Christine Gledhill illustrates the development of those structures from the 1940s thrillers in those of today. She shows that the alterations in the conventions reflect a continuing 'ideological struggle within patriarchy to maintain control over female sexuality and to assimilate its new, would-be liberating manifestations'; yet within this structure 'are enmeshed fragments that refer forcefully to the images and problems of a struggling feminism'. Her analysis of *Klute* demonstrates the need to place contemporary cinematic developments within the traditions that condition them.

All our writers except Janey Place consider these films noirs as a *genre* in one form or another — that is, in terms of thematic concern, narrative structure, iconography etc., a number of recognisable conventions run through them. Christine Gledhill, for example, writes:

> . . . genre production tended both to foreground convention and stereotypicality in order to gain instant audience recognition of its type — this is a Western, a Gangster, a Woman's Picture, etc. — and to institute a type of aesthetic play among the conventions in order to pose the audience with a question that would keep them coming back — not 'what is going to happen next?' to which they would already have the answer, but 'how?'

Janey Place, on the other hand, argues that because of the highly specific visual style and narrative concerns of film noir, its relatively short period (Sylvia Harvey suggests between *The Maltese Falcon* in 1941 and *Touch of*

1

Evil in 1958), and its appearance at a historical moment of crisis (post-World War II), these films – rather than constituting a genre, which is rarely defined in terms of a recognisable visual style and whose conventions very much bend with societal changes – instead represent a *movement* (p36).

However, in discussing the 70s film *Klute*, Christine Gledhill illustrates how the conventions of film noir have been employed in conjunction with traditions drawn from the European art movie to treat a 'modern theme'. This particular trend within the *thriller genre* can be seen in other 70s films and can be distinguished from the different permutation of the genre, of which Clint Eastwood's police thrillers are an example. In other words film noir can perhaps better be seen as a *sub-genre* or a *generic development* emerging from the earlier gangster genre than as a genre by itself.

Whether one sees this group of films as a genre or a movement, however, they are also very much products of Hollywood – even with its German Expressionist influences (Lang, for example) – and it is perhaps useful to signal here two terms used to refer to Hollywood films – 'the *classic text*' and 'the *classic genre film*'; while they are not necessarily mutually exclusive it is useful to bear in mind that there is a difference.

All the contributors in some way imply the notion of 'the classic film' in the sense of *genre*, by their reference to the visual/narrative/iconographic conventions through which one recognises a film to be of this group. (There is also a sense, in this term, of a perfect genre film against which others can be measured.)

The 'classic text' (applicable to genre and non-genre films) describes a *dominant mode of production*, which masks its own operation – either in terms of covering over ideological tension and contradiction, thereby giving dominance to a metadiscourse (see pp13 and 71), which represents the Truth *vis-a-vis* the film's content and meaning; or in terms of giving the impression that it gives access to the 'real world'. There is a continuing debate around this notion in terms of the mechanisms through which the metadiscourse/ Truth is carried and Christine Gledhill discusses aspects of it in relation to feminist film theory in the first part of her essay on *Klute*.

This particular period of the thriller genre – film noir – is, however, recognisably different from other films, in that where there is a metadiscourse, as discussed above, it exists at great cost, through considerable narrative and visual contortion. Film noir is particularly notable for its specific treatment of women. In the films of another genre, the western – for example, Ford's *My Darling Clementine* or *The Searchers* – women, in their fixed roles as wives, mothers, daughters, lovers, mistresses, whores, simply provide the background for the ideological work of the film which is carried out through men.

Since the placement of women in this way is so necessary to *patriarchy* as we know it, it follows that the displacement of women would disturb the patriarchal system, and provide a challenge to that world view. The *film noir world* is one in which women are central to the intrigue of the films, and are furthermore usually not placed safely in any of the familiar roles mentioned above. Defined by their sexuality, which is presented as desirable but dangerous to men, the women function as the obstacle to the male quest. The hero's success or not depends on the degree to which he can extricate himself from the woman's manipulations. Although the man is sometimes simply destroyed because he cannot resist the woman's lures (*Double Indemnity* is the best example), often the work of the film is the attempted restoration of order through the exposure and then destruction of the sexual, manipulating woman.

In her close visual analysis of a number of films noirs, Janey Place illustrates (through frame enlargements) some of the ways in which the dislocation of women from their 'proper place' under patriarchy is expressed visually. She shows the play on women's sexuality and sensuality, parts of their bodies focused on in their presentation as objects of desire. But women also visually dominate the men in many frames, reflecting the danger and the threat that they assume because of their overpowering sexuality, the control of which must equally be attempted in visual terms.

Clearly, as Sylvia Harvey shows, one way to evoke the threat of female sexuality is to exclude from the films that situation of the family in which it would otherwise be contained. Sylvia Harvey links the appearance of these films, with their new negative attitudes to the family, to the post-World War II period, when the previous ideology of national unity began to be eroded. The depressed peace-time economy brought an end to myths central to the American Dream and caused widespread disillusionment amongst veterans. There were also sudden fluctuations in the numbers of women entering (during the war) and then leaving (post-war) the job market. Thus the film noir *expresses* alienation, locates its cause squarely in the excesses of female sexuality ('natural' consequences of women's independence), and punishes that excess in order to re-place it within the patriarchal order.

It is largely because of this interplay of the notion of independent women *vis-a-vis* patriarchy that these films are of interest to feminist film theory. Christine Gledhill points out the problems genre films pose for feminists often caught between arguing against stereotyping, and therefore dismissing films clearly within the realm of artifice, and arguing for films which 'show women in real (i.e., recognisable) situations' – *Alice Doesn't Live Here Any More, Klute* . . . As she points out, the former position ignores the potentiality of genre films to play on ideological tension and contradiction; the latter ignores the existence of a 'realist' *aesthetic* (of 'the classic text' – applied not only to Hollywood, but also European art films), which equally structures tension and contradiction, but, as indicated above, is not seen to be doing so.

The theoretical project of identifying a mode of dominant ideological representation goes along with the impulse to find inconsistencies in a film through which ideological contradiction and tension may be seen to be manifested:

> Thus a criticism operating according to a perspective at odds with the ideology privileged as the film's 'message' or 'world-view' may be able to animate these effects to produce a progressive reading

3

of an apparently reactionary film, or (as I attempt with *Klute*) an ideological reading of an apparently radical film. (Christine Gledhill)

This brings us to the question of reading, which is clearly pertinent in the context of this monograph. There is no single position here on whether film noir as such is progressive or not. Both Christine Gledhill, in Part I of her essay, and Sylvia Harvey talk about both the *potential* progressiveness and the *potential* repression of film noir, the latter writer locating this potential in absence of *family relations* or their negative or distorted treatment.

Klute introduces the notion of family at the beginning of the film and shows how illicit sex has destroyed its unity; Mildred Pierce attempts to take over the place of the father as head of the family, thereby disturbing the balance of the 'normal' family unit; and in *Double Indemnity*, Phyllis Dietrichson has, we learn, already impaired the normal family unit by disposing of and then replacing the wife/mother, before she begins to destroy it by murdering her husband.

Through the operation of the film noir genre and European art film, writes Christine Gledhill, Bree, who is not a conventional *femme fatale* since she is *not* guilty of the family's or the man's destruction, can be saved from her own sexual confusion by Klute. And, writes Pam Cook,

> . . . through an explicit manipulation of genre conventions, by which a hierarchy of discourses is established, suppressing the female discourse in favour of the male; (and by,) on another level, the organisation of the narrative around complicated 'snares' and 'equivocations' (which) increases the desire for a resolution which represents the Truth . . .

Mildred Pierce is returned to her proper place within patriarchy (i.e., playing out the passage within patriarchal mythology from mother-right to father-right), since she too is innocent (the guilt of excess which she has initiated, is carred by Veda), but also because her husband finds his allotted place which she had attempted to take over.

It is interesting to compare the film noir, with its negative or absent family, with *melodrama*, a genre in which the family and its relations are the focus of ideological representation. While the family melodrama could be seen to deal with the ideological contradictions within patriarchy in terms of sexuality and patriarchal right within the family, the film noir as exemplified by *Double Indemnity* stresses precisely the ordering of sexuality and patriarchal right, the containment of sexual drives with patriarchy as Symbolic Order. Thus there is a sense in which film noir could be seen to close off the ideological contradictions of patriarchy which the family melodrama opens up. Using a framework of psychoanalytic theory, Claire Johnston shows that as the 'fault' in the Symbolic Order, woman must either be found guilty and punished (Barbara Stanwyck/Phyllis Dietrichson) or else restored as good object to her rightful place within patriarchy as a Symbolic Order — within familial relations. Alongside the work of placing woman within patriarchy can be seen the work of repression of homosexuality: considered abnormal and non-masculine — as Richard Dyer describes its operation in *Gilda* — and as

4

narcissistic identification (Neff) with the idealised father (Keyes) – as Claire Johnston discusses it in *Double Indemnity*.

One of the most important theoretical notions in a discussion of the classic text and of film noir is that of *discourse*, and a number of the contributions deal with the question here. It is particularly interesting where there is a discrepancy between one voice and another. For example, in *Mildred Pierce*, as Pam Cook points out, the Truth of the narrative does not reside in what we see and hear but in the Law which provides the missing information necessary to establish Mildred's innocence of the murder. We are torn between Mildred's apparent guilt of an actual crime and clear guilt of a crime against Patriarchy for which she must be made accountable to the Law, represented in the film by the detective, and the Symbolic Order of the Law of Patriarchy, manifested in the narrative structure and the use of lighting codes.

While Pam Cook claims that here the female discourse is totally relocated within the patriarchal order and, therefore, that the film lies *within* patriarchal ideology, my reading of *The Blue Gardenia* intends to show how the film establishes two conflicting discourses in the place of the normal monolithically male one of the traditional film noir. In allowing a space to Nora's discourse, Lang subverts the noir genre, and permits criticism and exposure of male attitudes toward women that the genre assumes. The progressive placing of women is revealed, as is also Nora's passivity in relation to male definitions of her. While in the end Nora herself has not moved beyond her placing in patriarchy, the work of the film has revealed to viewers the way men distort women and also offered a warning against too ready acceptance of male ways of seeing.

Richard Dyer, too, by referring to the interplay of genre, character and stars, is concerned, in his discussion of *Gilda*, to show that the female discourse, because of the use of Rita Hayworth and Glenn Ford, and because of the particular conjunction of voice-over and image, manifests itself in spite of the apparent control located in Ford/Johnny's voice-over.

The point about *Gilda's* use of Rita Hayworth and the character of Gilda herself is similarly made by Janey Place about a number of films noirs. Ultimately, she suggests, what we retain from many of these films is not the repressive treatment of women – in narrative and visual terms – but the strength of the image of the women in the face of textual repression. As she clearly recognises, however, it is important to understand the visual and narrative *work* of the repression of that image of women within film noir if we are to better understand the work of patriarchy and the possibilities for our work as feminists against it.

I wish to thank especially Sylvia Harvey, without whose initial work this book would not have emerged, and Angie Martin whose contribution has gone far beyond mere editing. Her thoughtful suggestions and constant support are largely responsible for the success of this project.

E. Ann Kaplan

Klute 1: a contemporary film noir and feminist criticism

Christine Gledhill

In the second part of this book I have attempted an analysis of *Klute* a recent 'new American cinema'[1] production starring Jane Fonda and supporting a reputedly 'liberated' heroine within a thriller plot structure – in terms of film noir. What my analysis attempts to describe is the ideological effect of the structural interaction between the two apparently contradictory film-making traditions implied in this description. On the one hand the film's modernity and seriousness of theme, linking prostitution, psychotherapy and the problem of woman, places it within a humanist realist tradition of European art cinema. On the other hand, the film's themes are cast within the plot structure and stylistic appeal of the noir thriller – an invocation of this period of the genre characteristic of the seventies – for example, *Chinatown* (Polanski, 1974), *The Long Goodbye* (Altman, 1973), *Farewell My Lovely* (Richards, 1975), *Marlowe* (Bogart, 1969).

As film noir has been largely discussed in terms of a highly elaborated visual style, of baroque stereotypes – among which a particularly virulent form of the *femme fatale* stands out – and of tangibly artificial, often incomprehensible plot structure, the capacity for *Klute* to make claims for the authenticity and progressiveness of what it says about women is worth investigating. Since my analysis is largely descriptive, what I want to do here is reflect on some of the problems such a film poses feminist film theory. These problems turn on the different ways the critical notions 'realism' and 'genre' have been taken up by ideological analysis both in film theory and feminist criticism.

The real world and fictional production

For much feminist criticism of the cinema — especially that coming from the Women's Movement rather than from a background of film study — the notions of realism and genre are totally opposed. While realism embraces such cultural values as 'real life', 'truth' or 'credibility', genre production holds negative connotations such as 'illusion', 'myth', 'conventionality', 'stereotypes'. The Hollywood genres represent the fictional elaboration of a patriarchal culture which produces macho heroes and a subordinate, demeaning and objectified place for women.[2]

In the first instance then, if feminist criticism is not simply to set generic convention against 'reality', yet at the same time is to avoid a formalism that evades the issue of society with the edict 'films refer to films', the problem it faces is how the operation of such conventions and stereotypes are to be understood in feminist terms — at what level their meanings and ideological effect are located.

At this point two different approaches emerge, the one deriving from a humanist literary tradition, the other arising from a more recent revival of Marxist aesthetics. Criticism deriving from liberal approaches to the humanities tends to treat an art product's fictional structures as providing aesthetic access to the work's truth which is then evaluated in terms of how it illuminates the world. In these terms conventions and stereotypes can be read metaphorically for their immanent meaning. In my later discussion of *Klute* I see Diane Giddis's analysis of the film[3] as an example of such a metaphoric treatment of genre. However, recent neo-Marxist developments in feminist film theory effectively reverse the values of 'real life' and stereotype, *changing the project of criticism from the discovery of meaning to that of uncovering the means of its production.* This change in direction is set out in Claire Johnston's seminal 'Women's Cinema as Counter-Cinema'[4] and informs much of the writing in this pamphlet.

In the first instance the aim of this new critical project is greater rigour and demands that closer attention be paid to the specificities of artistic production, and particularly how character is produced by other textual operations such as narration, plot, *mise en scene* etc. But it also implies investigation of a different order of meaning, something I will discuss in more detail shortly.

Behind this new perspective lies a change in the epistemological status of reality and fictional production respectively. In Marxist-feminist terms reality is understood not as phenomenal forms that present themselves to our immediate perceptions but as the historical product of socio-economic forces; it is a social product of which we, as feminists, our knowledge and ideas are an equally constructed part. To understand the real world then, it is not enough to observe life as it is lived on a day-to-day basis; nor can we call on the values preserved by human civilisation to penetrate phenomenal appearances. What we need is to conceptualise from a feminist standpoint the historical forces at work in the social formation which have produced and are continuing to produce both our material world and those phenomenal forms which appear to constitute reality.

Individual, concrete experience of oppression leads us to resist aspects of our world and provides the motive to interrogate it; but only the developing conceptual framework of feminism will enable us to locate the sources and assess the nature of patriarchy and so formulate the conditions necessary to change. In this sense feminist meaning is not immanent in the world waiting to be revealed. It is a social-sexual dynamic being produced by history.

Thus a change in the status of the real requires a corresponding change in conception of the aesthetic practice which seeks to represent the real. Language and signifying systems in general as part of a socially produced reality are similarly conceived as social products. Language, fiction and film are no longer treated as expressive tools reflecting a transparent reality, or a personal world view, or truths about the human condition; they are seen instead as socially-produced systems for signifying and organising reality, with their own specific histories and structures and so with their own capacity to produce the effects of meaning and values. Thus the 'convincing' character, the 'revealing' episode, or 'realistic' image of the world is not a simple reflection of 'real life', but a highly-mediated production of fictional practice.

A critical practice for which meaning is already constituted in the world, stored up in 'the highest achievements of mankind', is clearly dangerous for feminism, which understands such achievements as posited on the oppressive location of woman as the unknowable other, outside history, in the realm of nature and eternal truth, man's mysterious *alter ego* against whom he achieves his definition, and symbolically controls in artistic production. Thus it is arguably more important for feminist film criticism to analyse not what a film means in terms of its 'image of women' — measured against some supposedly objective reality or the critic's personal predilections — but rather those mediations which produce and place that image within the total fictional structure of the film with particular ideological effects.

In other words there are two levels at which meaning can be located: one as revelation read off metaphorically as the immanent content of the film's devices and style — of which I argue Diane Giddis's article is an example; the second as the set of structured effects produced by the dynamic interplay of the various aesthetic, semiotic and semantic processes which constitute the 'work' of the film. The second level of analysis asks, according to the now familiar phrase, not 'what is this film's meaning?', but 'how is its meaning produced?'

Whereas the first approach tends towards the validation of ideology in giving meaning the status of a 'truth', the latter attempts to locate behind the manifest themes of a film a second order of meaning which lies not in thematic coherence but rather in the implications the structural relationships of the text have for the place of woman in patriarchy. In other words the critic does not examine the relation between a narrative device, such as male voice-over, and the heroine for its equivalence to some symbolic meaning, but rather for the way it organises the female image into a patriarchal location. What this

8

shows us is not the expression of a truth individual women can translate in terms of an inner world, but rather an aspect of how patriarchy works. It is under this rubric that I have attempted my analysis of *Klute.*

The second point which emerges from the foregoing is the refusal to conceive of meaning as a static quantity residing inside the art work, waiting to be revealed by the ultimate, 'correct' interpretation. If meaning is a production, then the reader/critic plays a part in this production by bringing to bear on the work her/his own cultural knowledge and ideological perspective. A feminist reading re-works the text and produces meanings that would have been impossible prior to the development of the conceptual framework of feminism.

Within this context of a broad change in feminist film criticism, from the interpretation of immanent meaning to the interrogation of the production of meaning, I want now to look more closely at the way the opposition between realism and genre has been re-worked in neo-Marxist feminist aesthetics.

Bourgeois ideology, artistic practice and realism

In much recent theoretical work on cultural production,[5] the task of bourgeois ideology in Western capitalist society is seen as that of masking those socio-economic contradictions which are the driving force of history – the contradictions between the forces and relations of production and consequent division of the social formation into opposing class interests. The result of such masking is to obscure the fact of society as an interrelated totality grounded on contradiction, and as a historical and social production. In bourgeois ideology the members of the social formation find themselves as isolated individuals who confront over and against them society as a pre-constituted given which appears to derive from nature. The bourgeois concept of the human condition or of human nature thus serves to 'naturalise' and so put beyond human control those socio-economic forces which produce the social formation, and its contradictions. Besides masking the social origins of those contradictions, bourgeois ideology finds means to produce their illusory unification through such notions as the 'common interest'; or fundamentally antagonistic material contradictions are displaced onto idealist contradictions within bourgeois ideology which are amenable to resolution – such as the conflict between love and honour in neo-classical drama.

Having proposed the function of bourgeois ideology it is necessary to ask how this takes place in practice.

Ideology, in much recent cultural analysis, is understood in Althusser's terms as 'a system (with its own logic and rigour) of representations (images, myths, ideas or concepts, depending on the case) endowed with a historical existence and role within a given society.'[6] In other words, the work of masking, unifying or displacing contradiction goes on at one level in the circulation of pre-formed ideas, common-sense understandings, the conventional wisdom of a given social group or society. On another level, according to Althusser's arguments, this conventional wisdom is materialised in the way

9

we live our daily lives. If ideology is to be defined as a system of representations that have a material organisational force in society, the issue for film
theory is the role in this of art as a practice specifically developed for the
purposes of aesthetic representation and distinct from other forms of signifying practice.

In this context, the notion of a realist practice takes on a sinister aspect.
On one level the issue is: what is the epistemological status of the 'reality'
that the realist artist represents? Given that the 'representations' of bourgeois
ideology attempt to present reality as a phenomenal, unified, naturalised
entity to which the individual must adapt, there is clearly an ideological
pressure on the artistic producer to identify reality with the *status quo*. On
another level, if we grant this is frequently the case in so-called realist production, our task is to identify in particular realist practices those conventions
and devices which serve both to reproduce an ideological sense of reality –
masking and naturalising contradiction – and to mask their own work of
artistic production. Current film theory has developed an analysis of the so-
called classic text constituted in a monolithically conceived realism embracing
Hollywood genres, European art cinema and TV naturalism, which claims to
demonstrate how this inevitably and always takes place in any attempt to
represent reality. In the end the project of representation itself is said to be
based on the denial of contradiction.[7]

This is not the place to argue the pros and cons of a potential progressive
realist practice – something I feel needs urgently to be done. But what anti-
realist theory rightly draws attention to is that traditional humanist criticism,
which reads artistic texts in terms of their immanent revelation of the
meaning of life and the human condition, is reactionary in that it posits a
reality outside the action of social forces and so outside human control and
the possibility of change; and that the iconic media of the twentieth century
perpetuate this epistemology in the interests of the dominant ideology by
promulgating a natural view of themselves as a 'window on the world', or as
an expression of human life. It is in these terms that contemporary Hollywood's European look can be approached and similarly its need to take
account of the contemporary phenomenon of Women's Liberation.

Ideology, genre and subversion

What has been described above is in a sense the *ideal project* of the dominant
ideology in its attempt to turn artistic practice to its own ends. Realist
artistic practice clearly can provide ample ground for bourgeois ideology to
seed itself in because of the epistemological ambiguity surrounding the concept of 'reality'. However, due to a complex of contradictions in the socio-
economic and cultural conditions of the mass media and aesthetic production,
the hegemony of the dominant ideology is always in question. Despite the
claim that all mainstream production is tainted with realist reaction, genre has
been seized on by radical cultural analysts as the ground on which 'progressive' appropriations may be made of bourgeois and patriarchal products. It is

10

here that neo-Marxist aesthetic theory can make use of the specificities of fictional production which get lost in the description of the realist text as a form of production whose aim is precisely to disguise that fact.

The economic rationale of this compromise with the ideological requirements of 'realism' is found in the studio system. The formulaic plots, stereotypes and stylistic conventions of the different genres were developed in response to the needs of a mass industry to predict market demand in order to standardise and so stabilise production. A contradictory demand of the market, however, is for novelty, innovation. So unlike the concern with artistic exploration of the human condition which became the concern of the European art cinema, Hollywood genre production tended both to foreground convention and stereotypicality in order to gain instant audience recognition of its type – this is a Western, a Gangster, a Woman's Picture, etc. – and to institute a type of aesthetic play among the conventions in order to pose the audience with a question that would keep them coming back – not 'what is going to happen next?' to which they would already have the answer, but 'how?'.[8]

Thus genre provides neo-Marxist criticism with suitable territory on which to develop the more progressive possibilities of the notion of fictional production. Behind this approach lies the Russian formalist Victor Shklovsky's theory of 'art as device', in which he proposed that the function of aesthetic form should be to distort or 'make strange' everyday, 'normal' appearances, in order to impede our automatic perception of them, and so return them to our vision anew.[9] For Marxist aesthetics, because the means of artistic production are not simply formal devices any more than they are mere expressive devices, but rather determinate and determining structuring principles, Shklovsky's notion of 'making strange' is located in the contradictions that may arise between the structuring activity of art – which may produce its own effects of meaning – and the ideological themes of its subject matter. This is more likely to happen, however, where form is foregrounded rather than transparent.

In these terms the generic conventions and stereotypes of classic Hollywood can be seen as offering highly formalised and foregrounded sets of codes which can be set into play one against another, or against the grain of the film's thematic material, to expose the contradiction it is the film's project to unify, in a kind of *aesthetic subversion*.[10] Thus a criticism operating according to a perspective at odds with the ideology privileged as the film's 'message' or 'world-view' may be able to animate these effects to produce a progressive reading of an apparently reactionary film, or (as I attempt with *Klute*) an ideological reading of an apparently radical film.

Feminist readings of Hollywood genre

Claire Johnston and Pam Cook[11] have developed progressive feminist readings of this kind for the classic decades of Hollywood in the forties and fifties – the period of film noir. Possibly this period is particularly amenable to sub-

11

versive analysis in that what has been called the cinema's recapitulation of the embourgeoisement of the novel had reached the stage of discarding a purely emblematic and heroic mode of characterisation and event and was grappling with contemporary issues and larger themes in the interests of a more mature and demanding realism, but still within the confines of a highly codified studio-based mode of generic production.

For feminists such a formulation has interesting possibilities for analysis of patriarchal ideology in cultural production. The twentieth century has seen an acceleration in the process of the emancipation of women and an intensification of the contradictions surrounding the sexual division of labour and reproduction, so that women perhaps more crucially than before constitute a consciously perceived social problem. At the same time feminists have discerned how women occupy a tangential position in relation to production and culture, and, as guardians of reproduction, or a reserve labour force, or the mythical 'other' against which man takes his definition, are defined as constitutive functions in society rather than among its producers.

In such terms the attempt of much Hollywood production in its classic decades to handle the issue of women as a growing social force can be read as foregrounding the problem of the 'image' of woman not simply as a reflection of an economically constituted problem – the post-war impulse, for instance, to punish the independent female image as a reflex of the economy's need to push women out of production back into the home – but also as a crisis in the function of that image of defining male identity. Thus the analyses of Pam Cook and Claire Johnston seek to demonstrate how the attempt of the forties and fifties to produce the independent woman stereotype repeatedly founders against the role of the female image in the fictional and iconic systems of the cinema.

Character, discourse

The *progressive or subversive reading*, which shifts the focus of criticism from the interpretation of immanent meaning to analysis of the means of its production, seeks to locate not the 'image of woman' centred in character, but the woman's voice heard intermittently in the female discourse of the film.[12]

The problem for feminist analysis of the impulse of traditional criticism to locate meaning in character is first that it leads the critic into moralistic assessment of the heroine and her subjectivity in terms of its truth to the actual condition of women, or to supposed female aspiration, or to a feminist perspective on either. The problem with this is that ideological myths about women are as much a part of the real world as any other construct. Thus to use a particular individual's notion of 'the realistic' as a criterion of truth can only lead to disagreement, and if used simply to dismiss what is defined as stereotypical, to the elimination of the chance to examine the power of recognition which certain character structures or stereotypes may invoke.[13]

Second, as I have already suggested, the character becomes the dominant element in the text, the focus of its 'truth' in terms of which all other aesthetic structures are read. Such a procedure ignores the fact of character as a production of these mechanisms and of its structural location within the narrative.[14] As I hope to show in terms of film noir, these structural determinants can be crucial in affecting the degree or otherwise of ideological control over the character. If a positive heroine is to be created, who can speak from and for the woman's point of view, then there has to be a change in the structures of fictional production and these have first to be identified for their patriarchal determinations.

The concept of the *woman's discourse* avoids this collapse of text into character; it is equally valuable in that it cuts across the form/content division and similarly the division fiction/society. A discourse is shared by a socially constituted group of speakers or particular social practice, provides the terms of what can or cannot be said and includes all those items, aesthetic, semantic, ideological, social which can be said to speak for or refer to those whose discourse it is. It is to be distinguished from point of view in that the latter is attached to a particular character or authorial position, while a discourse stretches across the text through a variety of different articulations of which character is only one; it need not be coherent but can be broken by a number of shorter or longer gaps or silences.

A filmic text is composed of a variety of different discourses which may be organised along class, racial or gender lines, to name a few. The structural coherence of the text arises from the inter-relations of its discourses while ideological hegemony is gained by the power of the discourse carrying the dominant ideology to place and define the 'truth' of the others. Within patriarchal culture the various discourses that interweave through a specific text are so organised along gender lines as to give priority to the 'male discourse'. One form of subversion that feminists will look for then, are those moments when in the generic play of convention and stereotype the male discourse loses control and the woman's voice disrupts it, making its assumptions seem 'strange'. From this perspective the question the feminist critic asks, is not 'does this image of woman please me or not, do I identify with it or not?'[15] but rather of a particular conjuncture of plot device, character, dialogue or visual style: *what is being said about women here, who is speaking, for whom?*

Women and film noir

In this context film noir stands out as a phase in the development of the gangster/thriller of particular interest to feminist film criticism, which seeks to make progressive or subversive readings of Hollywood genre films. Film noir is a purely critical term (as opposed to an industrial category of studio production) and interest in the films it designates is itself fairly recent, arising as part of the sixties revaluation of classic Hollywood genres and concern with *mise en scène* as opposed to auteurs and thematic analysis.

Film noir is commonly identified as a particular period in the development of the thriller in the forties and fifties during which certain highly formalised

13

inflections of plot, character and visual style dominated at the expense of narrative coherence and comprehensible solution of a crime, the usual goal of the thriller/detective film. *Mise en scène* criticism has tended to interpret the aberrant style of film noir metaphorically, as aiming at the production of a certain mood – angst, despair, nihilism – within which are rearticulated perennial myths and motifs such as the deceptive play of appearance and reality, the eternal fascination and destructiveness of the *femme fatale*, the play of salvation and damnation.

However, my analysis, which follows, of the location of women in film noir will not attempt to interpret the genre's themes but rather to identify some of those devices, the effects of which structure, in an intermittent commentary, a discourse about women and sometimes, perhaps subversively, for women.

Five features of film noir

In my viewing experience there are five main structural features of film noir that together produce a specific location for women and somewhat ambiguous ideological effects. These are: 1) the investigative structure of the narrative; 2) plot devices such as voice-over or flashback, or frequently both; 3) proliferation of points of view; 4) frequent unstable characterisation of the heroine; 5) an 'expressionist' visual style and emphasis on sexuality in the photographing of women.

Investigative narrative structure

In the mainstream thriller the investigative structure presupposes a male hero in search of the truth about an event that either has already happened or is about to come to completion. This premiss has two consequences. The plots of the thriller/detective story offer a world of action defined in male terms; the locales, situations, iconography, violence are conventions connoting the male sphere. Women in this world tend to split into two categories: there are those who work on the fringes of the underworld and are defined by the male criminal ambience of the thriller – bar-flies, night-club singers, expensive mistresses, *femmes fatales*, and ruthless gold-diggers who marry and murder rich old men for their money; and then there are on the outer margins of this world, wives, long-suffering girl-friends, would-be fiancees who are victims of male crime, sometimes the objects of the hero's protection, and often points of vulnerability in his masculine armour. The second consequence is an epistemological one insofar as the investigation assumes truth to be a goal attainable by tracing a logical process of cause and effect, and that to every puzzle there is a key through which a complex but coherent pattern will emerge within seemingly anarchic events.

In the film noir cycle of thrillers both these features are inflected through the intervention of its other defining characteristics. To take the second first: the plots of noir thrillers are frequently impossible to fit together even when the criminal secret is discovered, partly through the interruptions to plot linearity and the breaks and frequent gaps in plot produced by the sometimes multiple use of flash-back, and partly because the processes of detection are for the most part displaced from the centre of the film by other features.

This brings us to the roles of women in the male world of the thriller, and to a kind of dual inflection of these roles, in which the norm of the bourgeois family becomes markedly absent and unattainable; at the same time as the female figure becomes more central in the plot than usual.[16] Frequently the female figure exists as a crucial feature within the dangerous criminal world which the hero struggles with in the course of his investigation, and as often as not constitutes the central problem in the unravelling of truth. Woman becomes the object of the hero's investigation. Thus the place of the female figure in the puzzle which the hero has to solve often displaces solution of the crime as the object of the plot; the processes of detection — following clues and deductive intellection — are submerged by the hero's relations with the women he meets and it is the vagaries of this relationship that determine the twists and turns of the plot.

Rather than the revelation of socio-economic patterns of political and financial power and corruption which mark the gangster/thriller, film noir probes the secrets of female sexuality and male desire within patterns of submission and dominance. Thus the enquiries of the police or private detective come eventually to concentrate on the state of the hero's, and more frequently, the heroine's, heart.

These inflections set up a conflict in the treatment of women in film noir. On the one hand their image is produced in the course of male investigation and moral judgement. On the other the suppression of the bourgeois family and centrality of women in the male world of action produces female representations outside family definition and dependency. This means questions of economic survival have to be broached. Two options are available to women — work or living off a man. In film noir both options emphasise the sexual objectification of women, for its criminal ambience situates working women in bars and night-clubs rather than in professions or factories. But sexuality and money are brought into explicit juxtaposition — a contradiction for bourgeois morality in that female sexuality is supposed to be sanctified by love given freely, which is hidden within marriage and the family. Moreover the heroine often shares the hard-boiled cynicism of the hero, which further undermines conventional sexual ideology. But this does not imply an unambiguously progressive approach in the noir treatment of women, for female sexuality is also juxtaposed within the investigative structure to the law and the voice of male judgement, and in many ways it is the underside of the bourgeois family that is brought to the surface for investigation.

One final feature of the investigatory structure of film noir consequent on its almost consistent use of flash-back is that the investigation need not necessarily be carried through the agency of police or private detective, but often takes the form of a confession either to another person (*Out of the Past, Double Indemnity*) or to oneself/the audience (*Detour, The Postman Always Rings Twice*).

Flash-back and voice-over

These two plot devices frequently work together in film noir, though their effects seem to remain the same even if they are used separately. The voice-over technique is usually an authoritative mode, either invoking the authority of the nineteenth century, omniscient story-teller (see *The Magnificent Ambersons*) or pronouncing with a documentary 'voice-of-God' (see *The House on 92nd Street*). However, within an investigative narrative with a flash-back — and sometimes multiple flash-back — structure, the voice-over loses some of its control over events which are locked in the past and which the investigative or confessional voice-over seeks to unravel.

Two consequences arise from this. First, the story-teller is put on much more of an equal footing with the audience, the temporal separation of the moment of telling and the event told leading to something of a dislocation between sound and image and leaving a gap within which an audience can judge between what they observe and the story-teller's account of it. This aspect is intensified in that the story-teller is often proved wrong by subsequent events and may even be lying (see *Gilda, Crossfire*). Second, the whole process of story-telling is itself foregrounded in the noir thriller in that the investigation proceeds through a complex web of stories told by the characters to each other or by the narrator to the audience.

Both these consequences are intensified by the fact that the centre of the plot is dominated by questions about female sexuality, and sexual relationships involving patterns of deception, seduction, and unrecognised revelations rather than by deductions of criminal activity from a web of clues. An extreme version of the story-telling structure of the film noir narrative is found in *Crossfire*, where three accounts of the same event are given, only one of which is true, and where, in a purely gratuitous scene, a mysterious and unidentified stranger offers to the hero three different versions of his relationship to the bar-hostess they are apparently both involved with, without ever confirming which if any of the stories is true.

One way of looking at the plot of the typical film noir is to see it as a struggle between different voices for control over the telling of the story. This feature of the noir thriller is important to feminist criticism and perhaps offers the key to a feminist analysis of this cycle of films.

In film noir the voice-over is generally male — (*Mildred Pierce* is a notable exception and very interesting for this reason, but it also represents an attempt to fuse two genres; the Woman's Film and the noir thriller) — something Molly Haskell sees as the ultimate sexist structure,[17] and it is true that in some versions of the cycle the heroine is almost totally robbed of a speaking voice (see *Laura*, where the possessor of the voice-over, Lydecker, struggles to retain control over his protégé's story against the investigations of the detective, McPhearson, who silences his controlling voice half-way through the film when he reveals the mistake on which Lydecker's version of Laura's story is based). However, the tendency of the flash-back structure to put a distance between the narrating voice-over and the story narrated also

means that a distance sometimes appears between the expressed male judgement and the woman who is being investigated and judged – leaving room for
the audience to experience at least an ambiguous response to the female
image and what is said about her. A good example of this is Gilda's strip
routine song 'Put the Blame on Mame, Boys' (in the film which is named after
her) which is discussed in this monograph by Richard Dyer (p95) and Janey
Place (p48).

Thus the woman's discourse may realise itself in a heroine's resistance to
the male control of her story, in the course of the film's narration. To be
clear, this has little to do with a conscious struggle on the part of the film's
characters but is to do with effects structured in by the interaction of
different generic and narrative conventions.

Point of view
Point of view may be a visual or a fictional factor in the cinema. In fiction the
term refers to the subjective perspective within which the story and its meaning is being conceived and from which the viewer should ideally interpret it.
This perspective may belong to the narrator, more difficult to identify in
films than in novels, to the consciousness of a particular character, or it may
be divided across several characters. In fiction where there are several different points of view operating, coherence and harmony are usually maintained
by one point of view carrying more weight than the others – often, in the
nineteenth century novel, the omniscient author's.

As was evident in the preceding discussion of voice-over, in film noir there
is a proliferation of points of view and a struggle within the text for one viewpoint to gain hegemony. For the image of women in these films this may have
a number of different implications. Where a single woman is seen from several
viewpoints – either by different characters (*Laura*) or at different moments
in time (*Double Indemnity, Out of the Past*) what is produced is a fractured,
incoherent image. This is taken up again in terms of characterisation below.

The struggle between different viewpoints may be between men for control of the image (*Laura*); or more usually in the forties noir thriller between
the man and the woman (*Gilda*). The generic features of the noir thriller
which locate strong women in image-producing roles – night-club singers,
hostesses, models etc. – encourage the creation of heroines whose means of
struggle is precisely the manipulation of the image which centuries of female
representations have provided.

Thus, though the heroines of film noir, by virtue of male control of the
voice-over, flash-back structure, are rarely accorded the full subjectivity and
fully expressed point of view of psychological realist fiction, yet their
performance of the roles accorded them in this form of male story-telling
foregrounds the fact of their image as an artifice and suggests another place
behind the image where the woman might be. So when in *Double Indemnity*,
Phyllis Dietrichson comes to Walter Neff's flat there is at least a sense of discrepancy between his vilification of her duplicity and the power of her sexual
appeal to him. In reverse, in *Out of the Past*. a similar discrepancy might seem

to arise between Jeff's sentimental romanticising of his first meeting with Kathie – 'She walked out of the moonlight' – and her 'playing' of the role.

Characterisation of the heroine

The material for the film noir heroine is drawn from the stereotypes of the *femme fatale* or evil woman and the good-bad girl, and generally contrasted in the film with a marginal female figure representing the good woman, worthy of being a wife, and often the victim. But the processes of narration in film noir described above modify this stereotypical material and the conventions of characterisation, particularly in terms of coherence and motivated development. The *femme fatale* is noted for changeability and treachery (see Sternberg's films with Marlene Dietrich). But in the noir thriller, where the male voice-over is not in control of the plot, and on the contrary represents a hero on a quest for truth, not only is the hero frequently not sure whether the woman is honest or a deceiver, but the heroine's characterisation is itself fractured so that it is not evident to the audience whether she fills the stereotype or not.

Rather than a coherent realisation of the unstable, treacherous woman, we tend to find in film noir a series of partial characterisations juxtaposed, not necessarily in continuity but separated by gaps in time (see *Out of the Past*) and often in blunt contradiction with each other. So, for instance, in *The Postman Always Rings Twice* Cora exhibits a remarkable series of unmotivated character switches and roles something as follows: 1) sex-bomb; 2) hardworking, ambitious woman; 3) loving playmate in an adulterous relationship; 4) fearful girl in need of protection; 5) victim of male power; 6) hard, ruthless murderess; 7) mother-to-be; 8) sacrifice to law.[18] Such a mode of characterisation, needless to say, is in marked contrast to the consistent moral trajectory of the male, who, although he may be confused or uncertain as to the relation of appearances and reality, at least maintains a consistency of values.

The ultimate ideological effect of this unstable and fractured characterisation of women depends on the organisation of each particular film. As an aspect of the genre's theatricality such characterisations contribute to the instability and uncertainty of the hero's world; to the ever deceiving flux of appearance and reality. In this sense they express a male existential anguish at the failure of masculine desire. But in the course of this, noir female characterisations, while they superficially confirm popular stereotypes about women, in their stylisation and play with the surfaces of the cinematic image they arguably foreground some of the features of that image. This is not to claim the progressiveness of the cycle but merely to assert its ideological interest for feminists.

Visual style

The visual style of film noir is commonly seen as its defining characteristic through which its formal excesses carry and submerge the incomprehensibility of plot and contradictoriness of characterisation – or rather turn these

18

features into a further expression of the existential angst carried by the films' 'expressionist' lighting-schemes and camera-angles.

Within this context the female image is frequently part of this visual environment just as she is part of the hostile world of the plot in which the hero is enmeshed. The noir heroine frequently emerges from shadows, her harsh white face, photographed without softening filters, part of the abstract lighting schemes. More crucially, of course, she is filmed for her sexuality. Introductory shots, which catch the hero's gaze, frequently place her at an angle above the onlooker, and sexuality is often signalled by a long, elegant leg. (*The Postman Always Rings Twice, Double Indemnity, Deadlier Than The Male*). Dress either emphasises sexuality — long be-sequined sheath dresses — or masculine independence and aggression — square, padded shoulders, bold striped suits.

Film noir — a subversive genre?

From this account of film noir we see that it exists in highly foregrounded generic terms, exhibiting as its principal features, conventionalisation, stylisation, theatricality, stereotypicality. As a sub-genre its mode has been described as determinedly anti-realist. To understand what produced this and its significance for women, it would be necessary to analyse the conjuncture of specific aesthetic, cultural and economic forces; on one hand the on-going production of the private-eye/thriller form of detective fiction; on the other the post-war drive to get women out of the work-force and return them to the domestic sphere; and finally the perennial myth of woman as threat to male control of the world and destroyer of male aspiration — forces which in cinematic terms interlock to form what we now think of as the aberrant style and world of film noir. What this means for women is the focusing of a number of contradictions, for the films both challenge the ideological hegemony of the family and in the end locate an oppressive and outcast place for women.

Klute and film noir

The issue, then, that my analysis of *Klute* will try to explore, is the relation between the claims made for the film in terms of a so-called progressive realism, and the potentially subversive elements it might incorporate in its recourse to the generic features of film noir. In fact the 'realism' of *Klute* is derived from a newly Europeanised Hollywood which, while it seeks stylishness — a certain cinematic elaboration on the surfaces of the contemporary world — also eschews the notion of the conventional, the stereotype and looks for a contemporary authenticity and psychological truth.

It is perhaps significant that its explicit generic affiliations are to a phase of the thriller that is firmly locked away in history. Their distance in time enables the noir conventions to be used less conventionally and more as metaphor and so to comply with the aesthetic needs of the European tradition which the film is assimilating. In this respect *Klute* joins other examples of

19

the recent noir revival such as *Chinatown* or *The Long Goodbye* whose Europeanised mode distinguishes them from the more orthodox line of development of the gangster/thriller into the Clint Eastwood police movie such as *Dirty Harry* or *Magnum Force*.

Such a view of the film's generic affiliation is supported by Pakula's account of his aims:

> At the outset *Klute* has all the characteristics of a forties thriller. For me, starting to direct quite late, the attraction was in using a genre for my own ends; it wasn't pastiche which interested me but, on the contrary, making a contemporary exploration through the slant of a classic form. What's also marvellous about the suspense film is it allows for stylisation or theatricalisation, which is not possible in more simple films like *The Sterile Cuckoo (Pookie)*.[19]

Thus the conventions, which in the classic film noir affect a structural distortion to plot and character and present a dislocated world, are now used consciously to offer a metaphoric revelation of a modern social and psychic malaise. What I will want to argue in my analysis of the significance of this for women is that under pressure of the psychologism of the European tradition the contradictions around woman animated by the dislocated world of film noir are thematically relocated and made amenable to resolution in the name of contemporary authenticity.

Notes

1. For a discussion of this notion, see Steve Neale, 'New Hollywood Cinema', *Screen*, v17 n2, Summer 1976, pp117-122.
2. For examples of early film criticism close to the Women's Movement and concerned with the opposition of generic stereotype and realism see the first issues of *Women and Film* (now discontinued). For instance, in the first issue, Christine Mohanna, in her article 'A One-Sided Story: Women in the Movies', poses against the stereotypes of male-dominated mass cinema – mostly Hollywood – individual 'works of art' – mostly European cinema – which support heroines, defined not in 'romantic or sexual terms' but in their own terms, as people. Thus Dreyer's 'The Passion of Joan of Arc', she says, 'evokes an image of woman so powerful it evades all stereotypes.'
3. Diane Giddis, 'The Divided Woman: Bree Daniels in *Klute*', *Women and Film* v1 ns 3/4, 1973, pp57-61; anthologised in Bill Nichols (ed.), *Movies and Methods*, University of California Press, Berkeley 1976.
4. Claire Johnston, 'Women's Cinema as Counter-Cinema' in *Notes on Women's Cinema, Screen* Pamphlet No. 2, SEFT, London 1973.
5. The account of bourgeois ideology given here is largely drawn from Stuart Hall, 'Culture, the Media and the "Ideological Effect" ', in James Curran *et al* (eds.), *Mass Communication and Society*, Edward Arnold, London 1977.
6. Louis Althusser, 'Marxism and Humanism', *For Marx*, Penguin, Harmondsworth 1969, p231.
7. For different examples of the anti-realist polemic see Paul Willemen, 'On Realism in the Cinema', *Screen*, v13 n1, Spring 1972; Colin MacCabe, 'Realism and the Cinema: Notes on some Brechtian Theses', *Screen*, v15 n2, Summer 1974; and Peter Wollen,

20

'*Vent d'est*: Counter-Cinema' in *Afterimage* 4, Autumn 1972. For a feminist development of this position see Eileen McGarry, 'Documentary, Realism and Women's Cinema', *Women and Film* v2 n7, Summer 1975; and *Camera Obscura* 1, Fall 1976.

8. For seminal accounts of the function of convention and stereotyping in the cinema see Erwin Panofsky, 'Style and Medium in the Moving Pictures', in Daniel Talbot (ed.), *Film: An Anthology*, University of California Press, Berkeley 1969; Robert Warshow, 'The Gangster as Tragic Hero', *The Immediate Experience*, Atheneum, New York 1970; and Lawrence Alloway, 'The Iconography of the Movies' in Ian Cameron (ed.), *Movie Reader*, November Books, London 1972.

9. Victor Shklovsky, 'Art as Technique' in Lee T. Lemon and Marion J. Reis (eds.), *Russian Formalist Criticism*, University of Nebraska Press, 1965.

10. For an early elaboration of a theory of ideological subversion in the cinema, see Jean-Louis Comolli and Jean Narboni, 'Cinema/Ideology/Criticism', translated in *Screen*, v12 n1, Spring 1971, and reprinted in *Screen Reader* 1. For a feminist adaptation, see Claire Johnston, 'Women's Cinema as Counter-Cinema' in Claire Johnston (ed.), *Notes on Women's Cinema*, op. cit.

11. See Claire Johnston and Pam Cook's essays in Claire Johnston (ed.), *The Work of Dorothy Arzner: Towards a Feminist Cinema*, BFI, London 1975; and Pam Cook, ' "Exploitation" Films and Feminism', *Screen*, v17 n2, Summer 1976.

12. See, for example, Claire Johnston's discussion of Dorothy Arzner in *The Work of Dorothy Arzner*, op. cit.

13. For discussion of the function and value of stereotypes for oppressed groups, see Richard Dyer, 'Stereotyping' in Richard Dyer (ed.), *Gays and Film*, BFI, London 1977.

14. See Richard Dyer, *Stars*, BFI, London 1978, which includes an account of the star image of Jane Fonda.

15. Julia Lesage comments on Joan Mellen's *Women and their Sexuality in the New Film*: '. . . Mellen rejects women characters she finds "unpleasant". Thus Chloe in Rohmer's *Chloe in the Afternoon* is "plain, with shaggy, unwashed hair falling in her eyes. Her complexion is sallow and unaided by make-up. Her sloppiness is intensified by a decrepit raincoat without style." ', 'Whose Heroines', *Jump Cut*, No. 1, May-June 1974, pp22-24.

16. See the article by Sylvia Harvey, 'Woman's place: the absent family in film noir', in this book.

17. Molly Haskell, *From Reverence to Rape*, Holt, Rinehart and Winston, New York 1974, p198: 'The guilt for sexual initiative, and faithlessness, was projected onto woman; she became the aggressor by male design and in male terms, and as seen by the male in highly subjective narratives, often recounted in the first person and using interior monologue, by which she was deprived of her point of view.'

18. Richard Dyer has analysed in detail the role of Lana Turner as Cora in *The Postman Always Rings Twice* in 'Four Films of Lana Turner', *Movie*, No. 25, Winter 1977/78.

19. Pakula: in 'Entretien avec Alan J. Pakula' by Michel Ciment in *Positif*, n36, March 1972, p36.

Woman's place:
the absent family of film noir

Sylvia Harvey

The world view generated within the film noir entitles this group of films to be considered as a distinct and separate entity within the history of American film.[1] What this world view reflects is a series of profound changes which, though they are not yet grasped or understood, are shaking the foundations of the established and therefore normal perceptions of the social order. Like an echo chamber, film noir captures and magnifies the rumbles that preceded one of those earthquakes in human history that shift the hidden foundations of a society, and that begin the displacement of its characteristic and dominant systems of values and beliefs. Like the world of Shakespeare's *King Lear*, in which the ingratitude of children towards their parents is at once the cause and effect of an immense disorder within the human universe, film noir offers us again and again examples of abnormal or monstrous behaviour, which defy the patterns established for human social interaction, and which hint at a series of radical and irresolvable contradictions buried deep within the total system of economic and social interactions that constitute the known world.

Despite the presence of most of the conventions of the dominant methods of film-making and story-telling: the impetus towards the resolution of the plot, the diffusion of tension, the circularity of a narrative that resolves all of the problems it encounters, the successful completion of the individual's quest, these methods do not, in the end, create the most significant contours of the cultural map of film noir. The defining contours of this group of films are the product of that which is abnormal and dissonant. And the dissonances, the sense of disorientation and unease, while frequently present at the level of plot and thematic development are, more importantly perhaps, always a function of the visual style of this group of films. Disequilibrium is the product of a style characterised by unbalanced and disturbing frame compositions, strong contrasts of light and dark, the prevalence of shadows and areas of darkness within the frame, the visual tension created by curious camera angles and so forth. Moreover, in film noir these strained compositions and angles are not merely embellishments or rhetorical flourishes, but form the semantic substance of the film. The visual dissonances that are characteristic of these films are the mark of those ideological contradictions that form the historical context out of which the films are produced.

This principled claim that seeks to establish the importance of style and *mise en scène* as, materially, that which produces meaning in these movies, is not to be adequately followed up in this article.[2] The piece attempts an approach to the problem of defining the contours of this group of films from a different angle.[3] The article, that is, tries to understand the process whereby the depiction of women in these films, by a complex and circuitous network of mediation, reflects such social changes as the increasing entry of women into the labour market.

It is the representation of the institution of the family, which in so many films serves as the mechanism whereby desire is fulfilled, or at least ideological equilibrium established, that in film noir serves as the vehicle for the expression of frustration. On the thematic level, one of the defining characteristics of film noir is to be found in its treatment of the family and family relations. However, there is another level of analysis beyond that of theme where things are not what they seem at the surface level of narrative and plot. One of the fundamental operations at this concealed level has to do with the non-fulfilment of desire. The way in which this underlying frustration or non-fulfilment is translated into, or expressed at, the thematic level in film noir is through the representation of romantic love relations, the family and family relations.

The repressed presence of intolerable contradictions, and the sense of uncertainty and confusion about the smooth functioning of the social environment, present at the level of style in film noir, can be seen also in the treatment of social institutions at the thematic level, and most notably in the treatment of the family. Moreover the kinds of tension characteristic of the portrayal of the family in these films suggest the beginnings of an attack on the dominant social values normally expressed through the representation of the family.

In so many of the major, and so-called 'non-political' American films, it is the family which has served a crucial function in inserting within the film narrative the established values of competitive, repressive and hierarchical relationships. The presence of the family has served to legitimate and naturalise these values: that is, to present them as the normal, natural and unthought premises for conducting one's life. Moreover, the representation of women has always been linked to this value-generating nexus of the family. The value of women on the market of social exchange has been to a large extent determined by the position of women within the structure of the family. Woman's place in the home determines her position in society, but also serves as a reflection of oppressive social relationships generally. As Engels suggested, within the family 'she is the proletarian, he the bourgeois.'

All movies express social values, or the erosion of these values, through the ways in which they depict both institutions and relations between people. Certain institutions are more revealing of social values and beliefs than others, and the family is perhaps one of the most significant of these institutions. For it is through the particular representations of the family in various movies that we are able to study the processes whereby existing social relations are rendered acceptable and valid.

Through its manifestation of a whole series of customs and beliefs, the family functions as one of the ideological cornerstones of Western industrial society. It embodies a range of traditional values: love of family, love of father (father/ruler), love of country, are intertwined concepts, and we may see the family as a microcosm containing within itself all of the patterns of dominance and submission that are characteristic of the larger society.

We might summarise here some of the most important concepts that are dealt with through and in the representation of the family. First, the concepts of reproduction and socialisation: the family is the arena that is sanctified by society for the reproduction and preliminary education of the human race, for the bringing up of children. In the free labour that it requires the mother to perform in raising the child, the family serves to legitimate a whole series of practices that oppress women. Moreover, in its hierarchical structure, with the father as the head, the mother as subservient, and the children as totally dependent, it offers us a legitimating model or metaphor for a hierarchical and authoritarian society. The internal, oppressive, often violent relations within the family present a mirror image of oppressive and violent relations between classes in the larger society.

Second, the family is sanctified as the acceptable location of a sexuality defined in extremely limited terms. Western industrial society has regarded marriage, and hence the family, as the only legitimate arena for the fulfilment of sexual needs, though this legitimacy has been somewhat modified to allow for the double standard, that is, for the separate codes of sexual practice to be adhered to by male and female. What is most interesting is that in general in the movies, as in society, the family at the same time legitimates and *conceals* sexuality. Although marriage is the only place where sexual activity is to be sanctioned, oddly enough (or perhaps it is not so odd) mothers and fathers are seldom represented as sexual partners, especially in those movies of the forties and fifties when censorship demanded that only bedrooms with separate beds were to be shown on the screen. So that, although married couples – that is, mothers and fathers – are the only ones allowed to engage in erotic activity, these parents or potential parents are normally presented in a totally de-eroticised way.

A final concept dealt with through the representation of the family is that of romantic love. Though so many movies go to extreme lengths to keep the two apart (a function of ideology working overtime to conceal its contradictions), romantic love and the institution of the family are logically and inevitably linked. The logical conclusion to that romantic love which seeks always the passionate and enduring love of a lifetime is the family, which

24

must serve as the point of termination and fulfilment of romance. And if successful romantic love leads inevitably in the direction of the stable institution of marriage, the point about film noir, by contrast, is that it is structured around the destruction or absence of romantic love and the family.

Moreover, since we are engaged in analysing the ideological systems of movies, and not those of novels or newspapers, it is important to note that in film noir it is not only at the level of plot and narrative resolution that lovers are not permitted to live happily ever after,[4] but it is at the additional and perhaps more important level of *mise en scène* or visual style that the physical environment of the lovers (whether created by landscape/set, or by camera angle, framing and lighting) is presented as threatening, disturbing, fragmented.

The ideological significance of lovers living happily ever after lies in the unspoken, and usually invisible, metamorphosis that is implied to take place at the end of every happy ending. By means of this metamorphosis lovers are transformed into fathers and mothers, into families. This magic circle of transformation is broken in film noir which, in presenting family relations as broken, perverted, peripheral or impossible founds itself upon the absence of the family.[5]

In certain ways, the representation of women in this group of films reflects the 'normal' status of women within contemporary social relations. The two most common types of women in film noir are the exciting, childless whores, or the boring, potentially childbearing sweethearts. However, in other respects, the normal representation of women as the founders of families undergoes an interesting displacement. For it is the strange and compelling absence of 'normal' family relations in these films that hints at important shifts in the position of women in American society. Among these changes must be listed the temporary but widespread introduction of women into the American labour force during World War II, and the changing economic and ideological function of the family that parallels the changing structures and goals of an increasingly monopolistic economy. These economic changes forced certain changes in the traditional organisation of the family; and the underlying sense of horror and uncertainty in film noir may be seen, in part, as an indirect response to this forcible assault on traditional family structures and the traditional and conservative values which they embodied. The astounding Mildred Pierce (*Mildred Pierce*, 1945), woman of the world, woman of business, and only secondarily a mother, is a good example of this disruption and displacement of the values of family life. The image of Mildred, in a masculine style of dress, holding her account books and looking *away* from her lover, typifies this kind of displacement (see p26).

The appearance of the early film noir coincides with the rise and fall of nationalistic ideologies generated by the period of total war. It may be argued that the ideology of national unity which was characteristic of the war period, and which tended to gloss over and conceal class divisions, began to falter and decay, to lose its credibility, once the war was over. The encounter with a depressed peace-time economy, with its threat of high prices and rising unemployment, began a process of general disillusionment for many of those return-

Mildred Pierce

ing home after the war, in search of those values which they had fought to
defend. It is this breakdown, also, this erosion of expectations, that finds its
way into the film noir by a series of complex transmutations. The hard facts
of economic life are transmuted, in these movies, into corresponding moods
and feelings. Thus the feelings of loss and alienation expressed by the characters in film noir can be seen as the product both of post-war depression and
of the reorganisation of the American economy.

With the increasing size of corporations, the growth of monopolies and the
accelerated elimination of small businesses it became increasingly hard for
even the petit bourgeoisie to continue to believe in certain dominant myths.
Foremost among these was the dream of equality of opportunity in business,
and of the God-given right of every man to be his own boss. Increasingly the
petit bourgeoisie were forced into selling their labour and working for the big
companies, instead of running their own businesses and working 'for themselves'. It is this factor of being forced to work according to the goals and purposes formulated *by someone else*, that accounts in large measure for the
feelings of alienation and helplessness in film noir.

It is no accident that Walter Neff in *Double Indemnity* (1944) seeks an
escape from the dull routine of the insurance company that he works for, in
an affair with the deadly and exotic Phyllis Dietrichson. The possession of
Phyllis Dietrichson, as of any of the other film noir women who function as
sexual commodities, is, in the magic world of the movies, held up as a tempt-

26

ing means of escape from the boredom and frustration of a routinised and alienated existence. Nor is it accidental that Neff, on his way up to his office to make his final confession, encounters the elevator man who tells him that he never could buy medical insurance from the company that he has worked for all of his life, because he has a bad heart. It is this feeling of being lost in a world of corporate values (represented in different films by big business, the police, the mob etc.) that are not sensitive to the needs and desires of the individual, that permeates film noir.

In the world of symbolic searches, exchanges and satisfactions created by these movies, women are accorded the function of an ideological safety valve, but this function is ambivalent. Presented as prizes, desirable objects, they seem to offer a temporary satisfaction to the men of film noir. In the (false) satisfactions that they represent, they might be seen to prevent the mood of despondency and loss, characteristic of these films, from being translated into an understanding and analysis of the conditions that *produce* the sense of alienation and loss. However, the ideological safety valve device that operates in the offering of women as sexual commodities, breaks down in probably most of these films, because the women are not, finally, possessed. Walter Neff (*Double Indemnity*) summarises the position of many of the film noir men when he concludes: 'I didn't get the woman and I didn't get the money'. The same statement would be true for the men of *Scarlet Street* (1945), *They Live By Night* (1949), *Sunset Boulevard* (1950), *Lady From Shanghai* (1949) and *Gun Crazy* (1949).

One of the recurrent themes of film noir is concerned with the loss of those satisfactions normally obtained through the possession of a wife and the presence of a family, though this theme is manifested in different ways. At the simple level of the organisation of the plot, *Woman in the Window* (1944) is one of the most obvious examples of the multifarious evils that befall a man who is left alone without his family. At the beginning of the film, the wife and children of the professor, who is the central character of the film, depart for a summer vacation, leaving him alone with only the company of his male friends. Left to his own devices he gets involved with a woman whose portrait, displayed in the window of a gallery, has mesmerised him. The woman turns out to be the mistress of another man, and because of his relationship with her, the professor is involved in a murder.

As he sits at home, terrified that the police are closing in on him, he is surrounded by the photographs of his family, which seem to reproach him for the life that he is leading while they are absent.

At the end of the movie we discover that these lurid events have been enacted only in the professor's dream. But it is none the less significant that this masochistic dream is triggered by the departure of the protagonist's wife and children. Moreover in the images of this departure (see p28) – the family farewells at the station – we are given certain visual clues about the operation of the marriage. The children in the foreground of the scene, engrossed in their comic books, ignore both their mother and father. The father fumbles awkwardly with his hat, the wife, with an extremely restrained gesture,

27

Woman in the Window

Scarlet Street

touches him with one hand; both clutch at objects (the hat, the pile of glossy magazines) which prevent them from embracing each other. There is no warmth in the farewell, no hint of the erotic. Even the polished marble floor adds an element of coldness to the scene.

In the world of film noir both men and women seek sexual satisfaction *outside* of marriage. This is true, for example, for the characters of *Woman in the Window, Double Indemnity* and *Lady From Shanghai*. However, a fundamental ideological contradiction rises to the surface in these movies, for the noir lovers are not permitted the socially acceptable practice of quiet 'adultery' (an ideological operation which, like that of prostitution, reconfirms the primacy of monogamy), rather they are required to carry out the violent destruction of the marriage bonds. Paradoxically (and it is through this paradox that the dominant ideology attempts to reassert itself), the destruction of the sanctity of marriage, most notable in *Double Indemnity*, results in placing the relationship of the lovers under such strain, so beyond the boundaries of conventional moral law, that the relationship becomes an impossibility, and transforms itself into the locus of mutual destruction.

In *Double Indemnity* the act of killing the husband serves as the supreme act of violence against family life, and has, in some sense, to be atoned for through the mutual destruction of the lovers in the macabre shoot-out, at the family house, which ends the film. It is perhaps most clear in this movie that the expression of sexuality and the institution of marriage are at odds with one another, and that both pleasure and death lie outside the safe circle of family relations.

Moreover there is clearly an impetus in film noir to transgress the boundaries of this circle; for the presence of husbands on crutches or in wheelchairs (*Double Indemnity, Lady From Shanghai*) suggests that impotence is somehow a normal component of the married state. Other imagery in these films suggests that a routinised boredom and a sense of stifling entrapment are characteristic of marriage. A large birdcage looms in the foreground of the family home in *Scarlet Street*, separating husband and wife (see p28), and the husband hovers uncertainly at the edge of the frame, holding in one hand the paint brushes which signify for him his escape into the fantasy world of his paintings. The family home in *Double Indemnity* is the place where three people who hate each other spend endlessly boring evenings together. The husband does not merely not notice his wife, he ignores her sexually; so that it is only under Neff's gaze that her long legs become the focal point of both the room as Neff sees it and the composition of the frame (see p30). While Neff looks at her, the husband looks at the insurance papers which function as his own death warrant, in the sense that they are the device through which the lovers plan to benefit from the large insurance payments on his death. Neff is subsequently caught up in the inescapable cycle of desire, death and retribution.

By contrast, the man in *Lady From Shanghai*, Michael, does not kill, and does not die, but neither is he satisfied. He watches as husband and wife kill each other (see p30), realising at last that she has betrayed him as well as her

Double Indemnity

Lady From Shanghai

husband. It is at the end of the movie a condition of the lonely and frustrating freedom of Michael (as well as for the crusading private eye in *The Maltese Falcon*, 1941) that he is not married, that marriage is an impossible state for him. The men of film noir tend to be the chief protagonists, the chief movers of the plot, the locus from which the point of view of the film proceeds, and the central narrative consciousness which retells the events of the past, and controls the unfolding of the tale. However, this dominance is not total. For the 'black widow' women, for example in *Double Indemnity* and *Lady From Shanghai*, are actively involved in the violent assault on the conventional values of family life.

If many of the films noirs depict a boredom and sterility associated with the married state, others present married couples who create a kind of anti-family. Most obviously, lovers on the run are unable to conform to the normal stereotypes of family or married behaviour. The lovers on the run of *Gun Crazy* and *They Live By Night* (1949) are, technically, married; they go through the marriage ceremony. However, their position outside the law does not permit them to function as normal couples acceptable to the dominant ideology. Their marriages function as the nexus of destruction, not as the showcase of desire fulfilled. Even the marriage ceremony has a slightly threatening quality to it in *They Live By Night*. The left foreground of the frame is taken up by the looming figure of the man performing the ceremony (see p32); the lovers face the camera in the centre and behind them, seeming to encircle and dominate them, hover the two stern-faced witnesses. Moreover the man who performs the ceremony appears again later in the film as the one who can most clearly foresee the rapid approach of the tragic end. In refusing with an unexpected honesty to take the money that he is offered to help the young couple across the border into Mexico, he is the one who makes clear to them, at last, the impossibility of their situation and the inevitability of a violent climax.

In *Gun Crazy* the isolation of the couple as well as their nonconformity to certain social norms is emphasised by the way in which they are presented as outsiders to the family and family life. Taking refuge with Bart's family at the end of the film, they so clearly do not belong; they constitute a violent eruption into the ordered patterns of family life. Moreover, as in *They Live By Night*, it is through the organisation of the *mise en scène* that their final doom is foretold. The scene in the deserted railway shack where they plan their final heist is characterised by a series of unsettling frame compositions: by such things as the obsessive presence in the composition of a large lamp, that dwarfs the human subjects; or by the blacking out of portions of the screen, caused by the intervention of objects in the foreground. As in *Double Indemnity* and *Lady From Shanghai*, the relationship of the lovers turns to mutual destructiveness. At the end of *Gun Crazy*, in the terrible dawn scene in the marshes, with the mist rising and the police encircling the couple, Bart shoots his wife in order to stop her from shooting his male friends – the cop and the newspaper man. Destructive passion characterises the central male/female relationship, while the more protective gestures of loving are exchanged, as in

They Live By Night

Sunset Boulevard

Double Indemnity, between men.

The sterility, in conventional family terms, of the central male/female relationships in film noir (and often these relationships are unfavourably contrasted with male/male relationships) is further emphasised by the childlessness of the couples. *Sunset Boulevard* offers an interesting example of this emphasis. The absence of the family and the failure of romantic love are central thematic elements. Joe Gillis, by becoming involved in the unsanctified relationship of gigolo (the paid and kept lover) to Norma Desmond, loses whatever chances he might have had of finding a successful romantic relationship. His failure is matched by hers, and the presence of the butler (von Stroheim), her ex-husband, now her servant, ministering to her relationships with men like Joe, is a permanent reminder of the failure of romance and marriage in her life. The macabre incident in which the butler and Norma officiate at the nocturnal, candle-lit burial of the chimpanzee which is, Norma's substitute for a child (see p32), seems to summarise the sterile state of a world which floats adrift from the normalcy of a society normally governed by the institution of marriage, and the relations of family life.

The family, within a capitalist economy, has functioned both objectively and subjectively as the locus of women's particular oppression. Its internal relations have *produced* those ideological entities: daughters, wives and mothers, that are so familiar a part of our world. It is the absence of normal family relations (of the network of relationships between mother-father-wife-husband-daughter-son) that forms one of the distinctive parameters of film noir. If we can say that familial *entities* are the ideological fictions called into being by family relations, then the absence of these *relations*, which are by definition normal in capitalist society, creates a vacuum that ideology abhors. This terrible absence of family relations allows for the production of the *seeds* of counter-ideologies. The absence or disfigurement of the family both calls attention to its own lack and to its own deformity, and may be seen to encourage the consideration of alternative institutions for the reproduction of social life. Despite the ritual punishment of acts of transgression, the vitality with which these acts are endowed produces an excess of meaning which cannot finally be contained. Narrative resolutions cannot recuperate their subversive significance.

Notes

1. The film noir period can be taken to coincide approximately with the appearance of *The Maltese Falcon* in 1941 and of *Touch of Evil* in 1958.
2. The polemic for this position, and for the primacy of this method, is developed in Bill Nichols' article: 'Style, Grammar and the Movies', *Film Quarterly*, Vol. XXVIII, No. 3, Spring 1975, pp33-49.
3. The methodological inadequacy of this article lies in its failure to conceptualise the relationship between its own (only partly articulated) method, and the primary hypothesis already postulated, namely that of the primacy of visual style. Moreover, the attempt at analysing ways in which certain structures within the movies reflect certain (changing) structures within the society that is contemporary with the movies is insufficiently theorised.

4. In a few of the films noirs, for example *Pick Up On South Street* (1953), the ending suggests that the lovers are to live happily ever after. However it can be argued that the mood created and the knowledge produced by the visual style of the film negates or undercuts the apparent happiness of the ending.
5. The notion of a 'structuring absence' is developed by the editors of *Cahiers du Cinéma* in their article on 'John Ford's *Young Mr. Lincoln*'; they write:

> What will be attempted here through a re-scansion of these films in a process of active reading, is to make them say what they have to say within what they leave unsaid, to reveal their constituent lacks . . . they are structuring absences, always displaced . . . the unsaid included in the said and necessary to its constitution.

(Cahiers du Cinéma, No. 223, 1970, translated in *Screen*, v13 n3, Autumn 1972, pp5-44 and reprinted in the *Screen Reader*, No. 1, 1978.)

Thanks for practical assistance to David Bradley (UCLA) and the Stills Department at the British Film Institute. Thanks for intellectual stimulus to members of the doctoral seminars in film, UCLA (on the basis of which work this article was originally written in 1975): Ron Abramson, Jacoba Atlas, Joe McInerney, Bill Nichols, Janey Place, Bob Rosen, Eileen Rossi and Alain Silver.

Women in film noir

Janey Place

The dark lady, the spider woman, the evil seductress who tempts man and brings about his destruction is among the oldest themes of art, literature, mythology and religion in Western culture. She is as old as Eve, and as current as today's movies, comic books and dime novels. She and her sister (or *alter ego*), the virgin, the mother, the innocent, the redeemer, form the two poles of female archetypes.

Film noir is a male fantasy, as is most of our art. Thus woman here as elsewhere is defined by her sexuality: the dark lady has access to it and the virgin does not. That men are not so deterministically delineated in their cultural and artistic portrayal is indicative of the phallocentric cultural viewpoint: women are defined *in relation to* men, and the centrality of sexuality in this definition is a key to understanding the position of women in our culture. The primary crime the 'liberated' woman is guilty of is refusing to be defined in such a way, and this refusal can be perversely seen (in art, or in life) as an attack on men's very existence. Film noir is hardly 'progressive' in these terms — it does not present us with role models who defy their fate and triumph over it. But it does give us one of the few periods of film in which women are active, not static symbols, are intelligent and powerful, if destructively so, and derive power, not weakness, from their sexuality.

Myth
Our popular culture functions as myth for our society: it both expresses and reproduces the ideologies necessary to the existence of the social structure. Mythology is remarkably responsive to changing needs in the society: in sex roles for example — when it was necessary for women to work in factories during World War II and then necessary to channel them back into the home after the war.*

*See the contributions to this volume by Sylvia Harvey and Pam Cook.

We can look at our historic film heroines to demonstrate these changing atttitudes: the strong women of 1940s films like Katharine Hepburn and Rosalind Russell (whose strength was none the less often expressed by their willingness to stand *behind* their men in the last reel) were replaced by the sex goddesses (Marilyn Monroe), virtuous wife types (Jane Wyman), and professional virgins (Doris Day) of the 1950s as the dominant cultural heroines. This is not to assert that these were the *only* popular movie stars of their times, but by the shift in relative importance of an archetype can be observed the corresponding change in the needs of the culture which produced them all.

Myth not only expresses dominant ideologies — it is also responsive to the *repressed* needs of the culture. It gives voice to the unacceptable archetypes as well: the myth of the sexually aggressive woman (or criminal man) first allows sensuous expression of that idea and then destroys it. And by its limited expression, ending in defeat, that unacceptable element is controlled. For example, we can see pornography as expressing unacceptable needs which are created by the culture itself, and allowed limited (degraded) expression to prevent these socially-induced tensions from erupting in a more dangerous form.

Two aspects of the portrayal of women in film noir are remarkable: first, the particular mix and versions of the more general archetypes that recur in films noirs; and second the style of that expression. Visually, film noir is fluid, sensual, extraordinarily expressive, making the sexually expressive woman, which is its dominant image of woman, extremely powerful. It is not their inevitable demise we remember but rather their strong, dangerous, and above all, exciting sexuality. In film noir we observe both the social action of myth which damns the sexual woman and all who become enmeshed by her, and a particularly potent stylistic presentation of the sexual strength of women which man fears. This operation of myth is so highly stylised and conventionalised that the final 'lesson' of the myth often fades into the background and we retain the image of the erotic, strong, unrepressed (if destructive) woman. The style of these films thus overwhelms their conventional narrative content, or interacts with it to produce a remarkably potent image of woman.

This expression of the myth of man's 'right' or need to control women sexually is in contrast to the dominant version of it in 'A' films of the 1930s, 1940s and 1950s, which held that women are so weak and incapable they need men's 'protection' to survive. In these films, it is the woman who is portrayed benefiting from her dependence on men; in film noir, it is clear that men need to control women's sexuality in order not to be destroyed by it. The dark woman of film noir had something her innocent sister lacked: access to her own sexuality (and thus to men's) and the power that this access unlocked.

Movement and genre
Any claims for film noir's special significance in portraying fear of women (which is both ancient and newly potent, today and during the period which

'It is not their inevitable demise we remember but rather their strong, dangerous, and above all, exciting sexuality.' Barbara Stanwyck in *Double Indemnity*.

produced film noir) must account for the particularly valid ties between film noir and the cultural obsessions of the United States during the 1940s and early 1950s. Film noir has been considered a genre, but it has more in common with previous film movements (e.g., German Expressionism, Soviet Socialist Realism, Italian Neo-Realism) and, in fact, touches every genre. For a consideration of women in film noir, this is more than a semantic dispute. Film movements occur in specific historical periods — at times of national stress and focus of energy. They express a consistency of both thematic and formal elements which makes them particularly expressive of those times, and are uniquely able to express the homogeneous hopes (Soviet Socialist Realism and Italian Neo-Realism) and fears (German Expressionism and film noir) brought to the fore by, for example, the upheaval of war.

The attitudes toward women evidenced in film noir — i.e., fear of loss of stability, identity and security — are reflective of the dominant feelings of the time.

Genres, on the other hand, exist through time: we have had westerns from the early 1900s and in spite of rises and falls in their popularity, westerns are with us today. Genres are more characterised by their subject matter and their iconography than movements, and they can express a wide and changing

37

range of ideologies. The convention of the railroad in the western, for example, has changed radically from 1924 (*The Iron Horse*) when it symbolised man's hopes for progress, the uniting of the continent, and the building of a peaceful community in the West, to 1972 (Sergio Leone's *Once Upon a Time in the West*), when it was the economic imperative causing exploitation of the poor. Many gangster pictures now champion the criminals and westerns depict the West as corrupt and lawless instead of an innocent refuge from corrupt Eastern values and a pure environment in which to build a virtuous society.

Unlike genres, defined by objects and subjects, but like other film movements, film noir is characterised by the remarkably homogeneous visual style with which it cuts across genres: this can be seen in the film noir influence on certain westerns, melodramas (even musicals) and particularly the detective genre. This style indicates a similarly homogeneous cultural attitude, and is only possible within an isolated time period, in a particular place, in response to a national crisis of some kind.

The characteristics of film noir style, however, are not 'rules' to be enforced,* nor are they necessarily the most important aspects of each film in which they appear; and no attempt to fix and categorise films will be very illuminating if it prescribes strict boundaries for a category. This leads to suppression of those elements which do not 'fit', and to exclusion of films which have strong links but equally strong differences from a particular category. Often the most exceptional examples of these films will be exceptional *because* of the deviations from the general 'norms' of the movement.

For example, in the classic film noir, *They Live By Night*, the strain of romanticism is far more important than that of the spider woman, who is in this film a minor character. The 'evil' Mattie who turns Bowie over to the police is even psychologically sympathetic – through love and loyalty to her imprisoned husband she is 'trading' Bowie for him. On the other hand, in as equally central a film, *Kiss Me Deadly*, no one, male or female, enjoys any of the transcending benefits of the romantic aspects of film noir. Only the victims Christina (Cloris Leachman) and Nick (the mechanic) are sympathetic: the rest are doomed only by their own greed. But after acknowledging that *every* film worth discussing is going to be 'exceptional' in *some* way and that their visual styles are going to vary, we can then go on to identify the visual and narrative themes that dominate film noir and influence countless other films made during the 1940s and early-to-middle 1950s in the United States.

---

* Often it is the films made from Raymond Chandler's novels, or films made by a director like Fritz Lang that have the most characteristic visual and narrative themes. Indeed, a film noir made by a strong director like Nicholas Ray may have more in common with one of his films that is not squarely in the film noir style than with other films noirs.

p.38 (top) '. . . the image of the erotic, strong, unrepressed (if destructive) woman.' Claire Trevor in *Farewell, My Lovely*.
(bottom): '. . . a particularly potent stylistic presentation of the sexual strength of women which man fears.' Jane Greer in *Out Of The Past*.

The detective/thriller genre whose subjects are generally the lawless underworld, the fringes of society, crimes of passion and of greed, is particularly
well-suited to the expression of film noir themes. The movement affected
other genres: melodrama particularly, but there are westerns and even
musicals that have distinctly noir elements. When the themes of the genre are
not conducive to the noir mood, an interesting and confused mix results.
Ramrod (1947, directed by Andre de Toth) is such a western. Veronica Lake
plays the typically aggressive, sexual 'dark lady' of film noir who causes the
murders; Arleen Whelan is her opposite, the nurturing stay-at-home good
woman. The usual stable moral environment of the typical western is lacking,
and the noir influence is evident in the murky moral confusion of the male
characters and in their inability to control the direction of the narrative.
Ramrod has the open, extreme long shots characteristic of the genre, but the
clarity they generally signify is undercut by the noir ambiguity.

The dominant world view expressed in film noir is paranoid, claustrophobic, hopeless, doomed, predetermined by the past, without clear moral or
personal identity. Man has been inexplicably uprooted from those values,
beliefs and endeavours that offer him meaning and stability, and in the almost
exclusively urban landscape of film noir (in pointed contrast to the pastoral,
idealised, remembered past) he is struggling for a foothold in a maze of right
and wrong. He has no reference points, no moral base from which to con-
fidently operate. Any previous framework is cut loose and morality becomes
relative, both externally (the world) and internally (the character and his
relations to his work, his friends, his sexuality). Values, like identities, are con-
constantly shifting and must be redefined at every turn. Nothing — especially
woman — is stable, nothing is dependable.

The visual style conveys this mood through expressive use of darkness:
both real, in predominantly underlit and night-time scenes, and psychologically through shadows and claustrophobic compositions which overwhelm the
character in exterior as well as interior settings. Characters (and we in the audience) are given little opportunity to orient themselves to the threatening and
shifting shadowy environment. Silhouettes, shadows, mirrors and reflections
(generally darker than the reflected person) indicate his lack of both unity
and control. They suggest a *doppelganger*, a dark ghost, *alter ego* or distorted
side of man's personality which will emerge in the dark street at night to
destroy him. The sexual, dangerous woman lives in this darkness, and is the
psychological expression of his own internal fears of sexuality, and his need
to control and repress it.

The characters and themes of the detective genre are ideal for film noir.
The moral and physical chaos is easily expressed in crime: the doomed, tor-
tured souls seem to be at home in the violent, unstable milieu of the underworld. The dark woman is comfortable in the world of cheap dives, shadowy
doorways and mysterious settings. The opposite archetype, the woman as

p.40 (top) '. . . expressive use of darkness.' *Double Indemnity*
(bottom): 'The dark woman is comfortable in the world of cheap dives, shadowy
doorways and mysterious settings.' Googie Withers in *Night And The City*

'a contrast to the fringe world': the family home in *The Big Heat*.

redeemer, as agent of integration for the hero into his environment and into himself, is found in the innocent victim who dies for the hero (*The Big Combo*), the longsuffering and faithful lover of the loser hero (*Pick-up on South Street, They Live By Night, Night and the City*) or as a contrast to the fringe world itself (*The Big Heat, On Dangerous Ground, Out of the Past*).

The Spider Woman

The meaning of any film image is a complex function of its visual qualities (composition, angle, lighting, screen size, camera movement, etc.), the content of the image (acting, stars, iconography, etc.), its juxtaposition to surrounding images, and the context of the narrative. Even more broadly, meaning is affected by ever-enlarging contexts, such as the conventions of a particular genre, of film generally, and of the time in which the film is made and in which it is viewed. It would be presumptuous and an impossible under-taking to attempt to establish a 'dictionary' of meanings within a system which is so bound for specific meaning to such complex elements and their interaction. Nevertheless, film noir is a movement, and as such is remarkably stylistically consistent. It thus becomes possible to identify recurrent visual motifs and their general range of meanings. Within these recurrent patterns, some drawn from conventions not specifically filmic, others specific to film generally, and still others to film noir or the detective film genre, the source and operation of the sexual woman's dangerous power is expressed visually.

42

The following illustrations are all comprised of these visual motifs, but the consistent meaning is not necessarily the entire meaning in any single image. A director — consciously or unconsciously — can use a convention against its usual meaning for expressive effect, as for example in *Laura*. The power to incite murder which is visually ascribed to Laura's magnificent portrait is revealed to be a product of the neuroses of the men around her, not of the power she wields. Norma Desmond in *Sunset Boulevard* is the most highly stylised 'spider woman' in all of film noir as she weaves a web to trap and finally destroy her young victim, but even as she visually dominates him, she is presented as caught by the same false value system. The huge house in which she controls camera movement and is constantly centre frame is also a hideous trap which requires from her the maintenance of the myth of her stardom: the contradiction between the reality and the myth pull her apart and finally drive her mad. The complete meaning of any single image is complex and multi-dimensional, but we can identify motifs whose meaning proceeds initially from common origins.

The source and the operation of the sexual woman's power and its danger to the male character is expressed visually both in the iconography of the image and in the visual style. The iconography is explicitly sexual, and often

Sunset Boulevard: Gloria Swanson as Norma Desmond emphasises the perverse, decaying side of film noir sexuality, with her claw-like hands, dark glasses and bizarre cigarette holder.

43

explicitly violent as well: long hair (blond or dark), makeup, and jewellery. Cigarettes with their wispy trails of smoke can become cues of dark and immoral sensuality, and the iconography of violence (primarily guns) is a specific symbol (as is perhaps the cigarette) of her 'unnatural' phallic power. The *femme fatale* is characterised by her long lovely legs: our first view of the elusive Velma in *Murder My Sweet (Farewell My Lovely)* and of Cora in *The Postman Always Rings Twice* is a significant, appreciative shot of their bare legs, a *directed* glance (so directed in the latter film that the shot begins on her calves, cuts to a shot of her whole body, cuts back to the man looking, then finally back to Lana Turner's turban-wrapped, angelic face) from the viewpoint of the male character who is to be seduced. In *Double Indemnity* Phyllis' legs (with a gold anklet significantly bearing her name) dominate Walter's and our own memory of her as the camera follows her descent down the stairs, framing only her spike heels and silk-stockinged calves. Dress — or lack of it — further defines the woman: Phyllis first is viewed in *Double Indemnity* wrapped in a towel,* and the sequinned, tight, black gown of the fantasy woman in *Woman in the Window* and the nameless 'dames' of film noir instantly convey the important information about them and their role in the film.

The strength of these women is expressed in the visual style by their dominance in composition, angle, camera movement and lighting. ** They are overwhelmingly the compositional focus, generally centre frame and/or in the foreground, or pulling focus to them in the background. They control camera movement, seeming to direct the camera (and the hero's gaze, with our own) irresistibly with them as they move. (In contrast, the 'good' women of film noir and many of the seduced, passive men are predominantly static, both within the frame and in their ability to motivate camera movement and composition.) The *femme fatale* ultimately loses physical movement, influence over camera movement, and is often actually or symbolically imprisoned by composition as control over her is exerted and expressed visually: sometimes behind visual bars (*The Maltese Falcon*), sometimes happy in the protection of a lover (*The Big Sleep*), often dead (*Murder My Sweet, Out of the Past, Gun Crazy, Kiss Me Deadly, Double Indemnity*), sometimes symbolically rendered impotent (*Sunset Boulevard*). The ideological operation of the myth (the absolute necessity of controlling the strong, sexual woman) is thus achieved by first demonstrating her dangerous power and its frightening results, then destroying it.

* See opposite.
** Lighting and chiaroscuro can express the moral relationship between characters; in the still of Phyllis Dietrichson and her stepdaughter from *Double Indemnity* the women are contrasted and morally characterised; see p.107.

p.44 (bottom): 'The moral and physical chaos is easily expressed in crime.' John Garfield and Lana Turner in *The Postman Always Rings Twice*. See also pp.58-9.

Often the original transgression of the dangerous lady of film noir (unlike the vamp seductress of the twenties) is ambition expressed metaphorically in her freedom of movement and visual dominance. This ambition is inappropriate to her status as a woman, and must be confined. She wants to be the owner of her own nightclub, not the owner's wife (*Night and the City*). She wants to be a star, not a recluse (*Sunset Boulevard*). She wants her husband's insurance money, not her comfortable, middle-class life (*Double Indemnity*). She wants the 'great whatsit', and ends up destroying the world (*Kiss Me Deadly*). She wants independence, and sets off a chain of murders (*Laura*). She wants to win a uninterested lover, and ends up killing him, herself, and two other people (*Angel Face*). She wants money, and succeeds only in destroying herself and the man who loves her (*Gun Crazy, The Killers*). She wants freedom from an oppressive relationship, and initiates events that lead to murder (*The Big Combo, The Postman Always Rings Twice*). Whether evil (*Double Indemnity, Gun Crazy, Kiss Me Deadly, Night and the City, The Maltese Falcon, The Postman Always Rings Twice*), or innocent (*Laura, The Big Combo*), her desire for freedom, wealth, or independence ignites the forces which threaten the hero.

Independence is her goal, but her nature is fundamentally and irredeemably sexual in film noir. The insistence on combining the two (aggressiveness

'. . . self-absorbed narcissism: the woman gazes at her own reflection in the mirror.' Rita Hayworth in *Gilda*. (See also p 61).

and sensuality) in a consequently dangerous woman is the central obsession of film noir, and the visual movement which indicates unacceptable activity in film noir women represents the man's own sexuality, which must be repressed and controlled if it is not to destroy him.

The independence which film noir women seek is often visually presented as self-absorbed narcissism: the woman gazes at her own reflection in the mirror, ignoring the man she will use to achieve her goals.* This attention to herself instead of the man is the obvious narrative transgression of Norma Desmond whose images – both reflected and pictures – dominate her mansion in *Sunset Boulevard.* She hires Joe Gillis to work on her script for her comeback, and she continues to insist he participate in her life rather than being interested in his. He dreams he is her pet chimp, and he actually becomes victim of her Salome. Joe finds an acceptable lover in Betty, the young woman who types while he dictates, smells like soap instead of perfume, dreams of *his* career, and is content to be behind the camera instead of in front. Self-interest over devotion to a man is often the original sin of the film noir woman and metaphor for the threat her sexuality represents to him.

Another possible meaning of the many mirror shots in film noir is to indicate women's duplicitous nature. They are visually split, thus not to be

'This attention to herself instead of the man is the obvious narrative transgression of Norma Desmond . . .' *Sunset Boulevard*

* See for example the still from *Double Indemnity* where Phyllis is putting on lipstick (p 104).

trusted. Further, this motif contributes to the murky confusion of film noir:
nothing and no one is what it seems. Compositions in which reflections are
stronger than the actual woman, or in which mirror images are seen in odd,
uncomfortable angles, help to create the mood of threat and fear.

In some films the 'spider women' prove not to be so and are thus redeemed. Gilda and Laura are validated as individuals (Gilda was simply acting
out the paranoid fantasies of her true love, Johnny and Laura was an innocent
catalyst for men's idealisations), but the images of sexual power they exhibit
are more powerful than the narrative 'explanation'. The image of Gilda we
remember is the close-up introduction to her, with long hair tossed back over
her head to reveal her beautiful face. Her song, 'Put the Blame on Mame,
Boys' (for every natural and economic disaster to hit the world) is ironic, but
stripping as she performs, the power she possesses as a sexually alive woman
seems almost up to the task. Laura's beautiful, dominating portrait that
haunts the characters and determines the action of the film when she is
believed dead is the strongest visual image even when she reappears alive.

The framed portrait of a woman is a common motif in film noir. Sometimes it is contrasted with the living woman: in *Night and the City* Helen is a nagging, ambitious, destructive bitch, but her husband gazes longingly at her 'safe' incarnation in the framed portrait — under control, static, and powerless. Laura's portrait is compositionally dominating, inciting Mark's fantasies and giving visual expression to Waldo's idealised vision of her, but only when she unexpectedly turns up alive does further trouble ensue as she refuses to conform to the fantasies inspired by the portrait. In *Woman in the Window*, an elderly, respectable professor puts his wife and children on a train, and longing for adventure, dreams a beautiful portrait comes to life and involves him in murder. He is about to take his own life when he wakes up, cured of his longing for adventure. The lesson is obvious: only in a controlled, impotent powerless form, powerless to move or act, is the sexual woman no threat to the film noir man.

On the rare occasions that the normal world of families, children, homes and domesticity appears in film noir it is either so fragile and ideal that we anxiously anticipate its destruction (*The Big Heat*), or, like the 'good' but boring women who contrast with the exciting, sexy *femmes fatales*, it is so dull and constricting that it offers no compelling alternative to the dangerous but exciting life on the fringe.

The nurturing woman

The opposite female archetype is also found in film noir: woman as redeemer. She offers the possibility of integration for the alienated, lost man into the stable world of secure values, roles and identities. She gives love, understanding (or at least forgiveness), asks very little in return (just that he come back to her) and is generally visually passive and static. Often, in order to offer this alternative to the nightmare landscape of film noir, she herself must not be a part of it. She is then linked to the pastoral environment of open spaces, light, and safety characterised by even, flat, high-key lighting. Often this is an idealised dream of the past and she exists only in memory, but sometimes this idealisation exists as a real alternative.

Out of the Past is one of the best of the latter type: one woman (Ann) is firmly rooted in the pastoral environment, static, undemanding and rather dull, while the other (Kathie) is exciting, criminal, very active and sexy. In this film the lack of excitement offered by the safe woman is so clearly contrasted with the sensual, passionate appeal of the other that the detective's destruction is inevitable. Kathie appears out of the misty haze of late afternoon in a little Mexican town, walking towards the detective hero as he sits in a bar, waiting for this woman whose image has already been set up for him by the man she shot and ran away from, who wants her back at any cost. They later embrace against the tumultuous sea, a sudden rainstorm, and the dark rich textures created by low-key lighting.

p 51 *Out Of The Past* (top) 'one woman (Ann) is firmly rooted in the pastoral environment.' (bottom): '. . . . the other (Kathie) is exciting, criminal, very active and sexy.'

50

The independent, active woman is often the primary noir element of noir-influenced films in other genres. In *Ramrod*, a western, and *Beyond the Forest*, a melodrama, the initial cause of the drama that results in death is a woman who will not 'stay at home' — Connie (Veronica Lake) on her father's ranch and Rosa (Bette Davis) in her small town with her doctor husband. Each woman is characterised sexually as aggressive and dangerous by the iconography and by the results of her actions. But because neither is centrally film noir, in *Ramrod* the quiet, waiting woman gets the man instead of aggressive Connie, and in *Beyond the Forest* Rosa's 'unnatural' ambition is powerful enough to cause only her own destruction. The intersection of the western and its noir influence is particularly interesting because in westerns women are generally genre objects representing home and stability rather than actors in the drama. Other examples of noir-influenced westerns are also characterised by active women and noir visual style: *Johnny Guitar, Rancho Notorious,* and *Forty Guns*.

The redemptive woman often represents or is part of a primal connection with nature and/or with the past, which are safe, static states rather than active, exciting ones, but she can sometimes offer the only transcendence possible in film noir. *They Live By Night* and *On Dangerous Ground* (both directed by Nicholas Ray, 1949 and 1950) are characterised by the darkly romantic element that can exist with the cynical. In the former film, the young lovers are doomed, but the possibility of their love transcends and redeems them both, and its failure criticises the urbanised world that will not let them live. Their happiest moments are outdoors in the sunlight, with 'normalcy' an ideal they can never realise because there is no place in the corrupt world for them. Mary (*On Dangerous Ground*) is not only cut off from the corruption of greed, money and power of the urban environment by living in a rural setting, she is further isolated (and purified) by her blindness. She teaches the badly disturbed and violent Jim to feel, and her reliance on him releases him from his emotional prison. Both characters are crippled — he emotionally and she physically — and need each other to achieve the wholeness of health. This interdependence keeps both characters and their relationship exciting, while other 'innocents' of film noir who exist only to contrast with the dangerous woman simply fade into forgetfulness.

Film noir contains versions of both extremes of the female archetypes, the deadly seductress and the rejuvenating redeemer. Its special significance lies in the combination of sensuality with activity and ambition which characterises the *femme fatale*, and in the mode of control that must be exerted to dominate her. She is not often won over and pacified by love for the hero, as is the strong heroine of the forties who is significantly less sexual than the

(top): *They Live By Night* Bowie and Keetchie are visually confined by lighting and composition as the outside world makes their love impossible.
(bottom): 'Mary *(On Dangerous Ground)* is . . . cut off from the corruption of greed, money and power of the urban environment by living in a rural setting.'

film noir woman. Indeed, her strength is emphasised by the general passivity and impotence which characterises the film noir male, making her a threat to him far greater than the career woman of the forties was, and thus only actual or symbolic destruction is an effective control. Even more significant is the form in which the 'spider woman's' strength and power is expressed: the visual style gives her such freedom of movement and dominance that it is her strength and sensual visual texture that is inevitably printed in our memory, not her ultimate destruction.

The tendency of popular culture to create narratives in which male fears are concretised in sexually aggressive women who must be destroyed is not specific to the forties to middle-fifties in the United States, but is seen today to a degree that might help to account for the sudden popularity of these films on college campuses, television, and film retrospectives. But despite their regressive ideological function on a strictly narrative level, a fuller explanation for the current surge of interest in film noir must acknowledge its uniquely sensual visual style which often overwhelms (or at least acts upon) the narrative so compellingly that it stands as the only period in American film in which women are deadly but sexy, exciting, and strong.

A note on illustrations pp. 55-67
The stills that follow provide further illustrations of the stylistic and iconographical motifs identified in Janey Place's article. They fall into eight groups:
I   'the iconography is explicitly sexual . . . : long hair (blond or dark), makeup and jewellery.' p.55.
II 'Cigarettes with their wispy trails of smoke can become cues of dark and immoral sensuality.' p.56.
III 'Dress − or lack of it − . . . defines the woman.' p.57.
IV 'the iconography of violence (primarily guns) is a specific symbol . . of her "unnatural" phallic power.' p.58-9.
V   'The framed portrait of a woman is a common motif in film noir.' p.60.
VI Mirrors indicate narcissism or duplicity. p.61
VII Women 'are overwhelmingly the compositional focus, generally centre frame and/or in the foreground or pulling focus to them in the background. They control camera movement, seeming to direct the camera (and the hero's gaze, with our own) irresistibly with them as they move.' pp. 62-4. In the shot from *Gilda* on p.64, Gilda's mere presence in the house throws a shadow over Johnny as he approaches.
VIII 'The visual style conveys . . . mood through expressive use of darkness: both real, in predominantly underlit and night-time scenes, and psychologically through shadows and claustrophobic compositions which overwhelm the character in exterior as well as interior settings . . . The sexual, dangerous woman lives in this darkness.' pp.65-7

Googie Withers in *Night And The City*

Ava Gardner in *The Killers*

Jean Peters in *Pick-up On South Street*

Rita Hayworth in *Gilda*

56

Gloria Grahame in *The Big Heat*

Rita Hayworth in *Gilda*

Gaby Rodgers in *Kiss Me Deadly*

Rita Hayworth in *Lady From Shanghai*

Jane Greer in *Out of the Past*

Gloria Grahame in *The Big Heat*

59

Gloria Swanson's portrait comes between William Holden and Nancy Olson in *Sunset Boulevard.*

Joan Bennett in *Woman In The Window*

Gloria Grahame in *The Big Heat*

Rita Hayworth in *Lady From Shanghai*

61

Jane Greer in *Out Of The Past*

Rita Hayworth in *Gilda*

Barbara Stanwyck in *Double Indemnity*

Googie Withers in *Night And The City*

Glenn Ford in *Gilda*

Barbara Stanwyck in *Double Indemnity*

Gloria Swanson in *Sunset Boulevard*

Jane Greer in *Out Of The Past*

Gloria Grahame in *The Big Heat*

Jeannette Nolan in *The Big Heat*

Duplicity in *Mildred Pierce*

Pam Cook

> We live in a society ruled by the father, in which the place of the
> mother is suppressed. Motherhood and how to live it, or not to live
> it, lies at the roots of the dilemma.
>
> Laura Mulvey in *Riddles of the Sphinx:* a film by Laura Mulvey and
> Peter Wollen, *Screen,* v18 n2, Summer 1977.

To write about *Mildred Pierce* as an example of film noir poses more
problems than are immediately apparent. In spite of the fact that several
articles about the film[1] place it as typical of the 1940s genre characterised
by a prevailing mood of pessimism and paranoia, a visual style dependent
upon 'expressionist' lighting and decor, systematic use of geometric patterns
of light and shadow, distortion produced through camera angles and wide-
angle lenses and a convoluted organisation of narrative, *Mildred Pierce* does
not fit easily into the self-contained, homogeneous world created by those
formal strategies now accepted as characteristic of film noir.[2]

The difficulties of establishing and maintaining the boundaries of genre
are obvious. Elements of film noir can be found in films as far removed in
time and place as *Pursued* (Raoul Walsh 1947), *Vampyr* (Carl Dreyer 1932)
and *Nostalgia* (Hollis Frampton 1971). It is not the intention of this article
to discuss *Mildred Pierce* in terms of the representation of women in film
noir, nor to try to prove that the film is not a good example of film noir.
I would claim instead that the film deals explicitly with questions of genre
as part of its project, that the ideological work of the film is to articulate the
necessity for the drawing of boundaries and to encourage the acceptance of
the repression which the establishment of such an order entails. *Mildred
Pierce* is interesting for the ways in which it signifies its problematic: the
historical need to re-construct an economy based on a division of labour by
which men command the means of production and women remain within the
family, in other words the need to re-construct a failing patriarchal order.
This re-construction work is problematic precisely because it is based on the
brutal and enforced repression of female sexuality, and the institutionalisa-
tion of a social place for both men (as fathers and husbands) and women (as

mothers and wives) which rests uneasily on this repression, aware of the continual possibility of the eruption into the present of the submerged past.

On one level this work of repression is signified through an explicit manipulation of genre conventions, by which a hierarchy of discourses is established, suppressing the female discourse in favour of the male; on another level, by the organisation of the narrative around complicated 'snares' and 'equivocations' to increase the desire for a resolution which represents the Truth, whatever the cost. On every level the film works on audience expectation and response in order to produce audience subject positions based on defence, and elements of these positions are necessarily retained, even in the face of the re-establishment of Order and Truth, thus emphasising the need for work, sacrifice and suffering in the process of re-construction. The aim of this article is to suggest some of the ways in which *Mildred Pierce* articulates this problematic, avoiding if possible the idea that the film simply reflects the historical needs of post-war America. The drama of the institution of the patriarchal order, the familiar Oedipal story, is enacted and re-enacted throughout history in many and various forms; in the context of the transition to a post-war economy, an impaired masculine population, the disintegration of the family unit and the increased economic and sexual independence of women, the Oedipal structure is threatened: the system which gives men and women their place in society must be reconstructed by a more explicit work of repression, and the necessity for this repression must be established unequivocally, by resolving equivocation. The ideological work of the film then is the way in which it articulates its project, encouraging certain subject positions rather than others, signifying a problem which is not only specific to *Mildred Pierce* itself, and the conditions in which it was produced, but also general in so far as the institution of patriarchy is an historical problem.

The extent of the problem of the institution of patriarchy is indicated in the work of J.J. Bachofen,[3] who, in his scholarly and imaginative study of ancient myths and symbolism traces the historical transition from mother-right to father-right, a transition articulated by a number of myths of which the Oedipus story is only one. From his studies Bachofen insists that there is universal evidence for the historical existence of a matriarchal society which preceded our patriarchal system, a claim which has brought his ideas into question.[4] Nevertheless his work remains fascinating for its revelation of the extent to which the idea of a society based on mother-right persists in mythology, a society which was forcibly overturned in the transition to a 'higher' form of civilisation: patriarchy. I would argue that *Mildred Pierce* draws extensively on this mythology, and on the symbolism which Bachofen identifies as specific to the myth: that the project of the film is to re-present the violent overthrow of mother-right in favour of father-right[5] through the symbolic use of film lighting and the organisation of its narrative structure.

In an interesting article on *Mildred Pierce*,[6] Joyce Nelson discusses the film in terms of its narrative structure, drawing attention to the device of the 'false suture'* used to structure audience response, to lead the audience to concentrate on the need to resolve the enigma rather than to speculate on the possibility of alternative readings. The 'false suture' involves the masking, through the work of other filmic and cinematic codes, of the exclusion of a reverse-shot in order to create an enigma which the film will answer for the viewer, later, in the final flashback, when the missing shot is re-inserted and the truth about the murder is revealed.

Nelson points out an apparently obvious fact, which is nevertheless not always mentioned in discussions of the film as film noir: the scenes which take place in the present are significantly more suggestive of film noir than are the two segments comprising Mildred's version of her own story. She goes on to show that Mildred's discourse is markedly different from the framing discourse of the detective, in that he is simply concerned with establishing the Truth, with resolving the enigma, while Mildred's story contains complexity and ambiguity, showing a concern for feelings rather than facts. The detective's discourse is directed towards cleaning up the past, and this involves the invalidation of Mildred's version of the story, in terms of form *and* content. At the end of the second flashback the detective reveals that he knew the truth all the time, that Mildred was 'only the key'. This initiates the final flashback in which the enigma is resolved, shot almost entirely in noir style (see below).

Nelson goes on to discuss the representation in the film of the relationship of similarity between Veda and Mildred, suggesting that the film asks us, through the device of metaphorical substitution, to confuse the wicked Veda with the honest Mildred, thus establishing Mildred's innate guilt, even though she is not guilty of the actual murder.

I find Joyce Nelson's reading of *Mildred Pierce* interesting because it uses a theoretical approach which assumes that the ideological work of the film lies in its structure, and in the structures in which it engages its audience. Although I disagree with some of her conclusions, this reading offers some useful insights into *Mildred Pierce* which I should like to use as a starting point for my own discussion of the film, and develop a little further. I shall draw on the structure of the film itself, its use of narrative and filmic codes of lighting, but also on those non-cinematic elements already indicated: the mythology outlined by Bachofen, and the sexual structure of the Oedipus complex appropriated from mythology by Freud. What follows is not intended to be a textual analysis; rather I am trying to suggest a way of reading the film which opens up the question of the working of patriarchal ideology and the place it holds for women and men, and the implications of this question for sexual politics as well as for feminist film criticism.

* Nelson takes the term 'suture' from the influential article by Daniel Dayan: 'The Tutor-Code of Classical Cinema', in *Film Quarterly*, Fall 1974. The concept has been the subject of much debate (see 'Notes on Suture' by Stephen Heath in *Screen*, v18 n4), but can be briefly defined as the system by which, in classic cinema, the spectator is bound into the image-frame and narrative.

Mildred Pierce and genre

As I indicated in my opening paragraph, the film does not fit easily into the category of film noir. Although the opening and closing sequences, and two short interruptions during the film, are shot in 'classic' noir style, the first two long flashback sequences in which Mildred tells the story of her past are significantly different, more evenly lit, few variations in camera angle, etc., except towards the end of the second flashback when Mildred realises that Monty has betrayed her and she 'confesses' to the murder, when noir *mise en scène* takes over Mildred's discourse as well. The first flashback sequences are also concerned with different subject matter: the family, sexual and emotional relationships, property, work and investment. Mildred's discourse is the discourse of melodrama, her story is the stuff of which the 'Woman's Picture' was made in the pre-war and war years when women were seen to have an active part to play in society and the problems of passion, desire and emotional excess articulated by melodrama[7] could be tolerated. The difference between the two forms of discourse (Mildred's story and the framing noir discourse) is marked enough for some account of the function of this marking to be necessary.

It seems that a basic split is created in the film between melodrama and film noir, between 'Woman's Picture' and 'Man's Film', a split which indicates the presence of two 'voices', female and male, which in itself is a mark of excess since 'classic' film is generally characterised by the dominance of a metadiscourse, which represents the Truth. *Mildred Pierce* is constituted as a sexually ambiguous film, an ambiguity founded on duplicity which is eventually resolved by the re-assertion of the patriarchal metadiscourse. In the process of resolution, melodrama, Mildred's point of view, is displaced by film noir (in which female discourse is suppressed but remains in the form of threatening shadows and man-killing Amazonian women), when in the final flashback narrative and lighting codes combine with extreme camera angles and music to connote imminent chaos, and the truth about Monty's murder is revealed. The consequences of the retreat from patriarchy are represented as the complete upheaval of social order leading to betrayal and death, in the face of which the reconstitution of the patriarchal order is seen to be a necessary defence.

The question of the retreat from patriarchy brings me to Bachofen's theory of the relationship between mother-right and father-right. From his study of myth he establishes two basic cultural levels: a primitive level of swamp generation where the union of water and land brings about birth which swiftly becomes death and returns to the land. This level is telluric, associated with sexual promiscuity and characterised as female. The second level is luminous and transcendent, associated with light and the sun, a higher intellectual and spiritual level, characterised as male. The second (patriarchal) level is the one to which all human life aspires, and therefore the more primitive level (called hetaerism by Bachofen) must constantly be overcome. The schema is more complex than this, taking in various stages between the two levels. Demetrian matriarchy, for instance, occupies a position midway bet-

Mise en scène in melodrama.

Mise en scène in film noir.

ween hetaerism and patriarchy, and is therefore an area of struggle since it stands in opposition both to the excesses of hetaerism and to the institution of patriarchy, which signals the loss of matriarchal rights and privileges. In the transition from mother-right to father-right there is a further stage: the Dionysian, which heralds the founding of patriarchy, undermining the Demetrian principle by an alliance with hetaerism and a return to the sensual frenzy of a more primitive era, characterised as an era of sexual freedom in which women are held in common by men. Against the abuse of women's bodies which hetaerism implies the man-killing Amazon arises, yet another stage in the transition to patriarchy.

Bachofen isolates a symbolic grid which supports the basic division between female (matriarchal)/male (patriarchal), a shortened version of which could be set out as follows:

Female	Male
Tellurian	Uranian
Material/Corporeal	Spiritual/Intellectual
Night	Day
Dark	Light
Passive	Active
Left	Right
Mass solidarity	Individuality
Womb	Phallus

It is not arbitrary to apply Bachofen's schema of the struggle between mother-right and father-right to *Mildred Pierce*. Apart from the film's thematic concern with a mother who attempts to gain control of family and business, the classic struggle between Mother and Father, and its 'inevitable' resolution is multiply coded in the film in the narrative organisation and the symbolic use of film lighting.

Film noir

In accordance with Bachofen's schema the contrast dark/light in the film noir sections of *Mildred Pierce* is taken to connote sexual ambiguity: the presence of male and female in the text, the struggle between two symbolic orders. In film noir generally, the protagonist, usually male, moves unhappily through this world of sexual ambiguity (against which his paranoia is a defence) until it is resolved, either by his own death at the hands of the Father, or by his taking over from the Father as the agent of death. Although there are exceptions, women who are represented as the agents of death usually turn out to be only instruments when the duplicity is resolved by the narrative. It is unusual for film noir to have a female protagonist narrating her own story; in *Mildred Pierce* Mildred's story is revealed as duplicitous, thus foregrounding the work of repression involved in narrative resolution.

As already indicated, the noir sections of the film are situated in the present, a present therefore characterised by violence and death, uncertainty and duplicity. Duplicity is underlined in the text of the film by the use of contrasting light and shadow and by the use of a 'snare' in the narrative: the exclusion of the reverse shot which would reveal the true murderer encourages the audience to believe that Mildred is the murderer/agent of death, especially when, in true noir heroine style, she proceeds to set Wally Fay up as the murderer, apparently to protect herself, using her sexuality as bait. 'You make me shiver, Mildred', says Wally, reinforcing the belief that it is Mildred who is the location of duplicity.

Later, at the police station, the brisk, orderly atmosphere makes Mildred nervous as she waits to be questioned: again she is seen as the location of uncertainty, this time in the face of the Law which will tolerate no uncertainty or ambiguity.

The first flashback ends at the point where Mildred is at the height of her economic success and Bert gives her the divorce she wanted. We return to the present in the police station, and the lighting (shadows) on Mildred's face suggest her guilt in the present when she has just been seen as successful in her own right in the past. The function of this interruption seems to be to encourage the audience to anticipate the fate of independent successful career women, and to force a separation or distance between audience and any sympathy or identification with Mildred's success. Towards the end of the second flashback, when Mildred's story draws to its (false) conclusion and closer to present time (when the murder takes place), deceit and betrayal, represented by Wally, Veda and Monty are rife, and Mildred has lost everything that was dear to her. Film noir conventions invade Mildred's discourse and she confesses to the murder.

Mildred's confession does not introduce any contradiction into her discourse. On the contrary, it allows her to insert herself into the present as a woman still in control of her destiny, with the power of death over the men who betray her. In the face of this assertion of power, based on duplicity, since Mildred is not the real murderer, the detective's response is to remove all possibility of duplicity by invalidating Mildred's confession. He reveals the truth, which he knew all the time anyway, confronting Mildred with Veda, who confesses, believing that Mildred has betrayed her, and is taken away from Mildred into the custody of the Law.

In this final cleaning-up process all power is seen to return into the hands of the Law. The paternalistic detective, who has secretly always controlled the progress of the narrative because of his foreknowledge of the truth, dispels duplicity by throwing light upon the scene: his assertion of the Truth is supported symbolically when he opens the blinds to let in the dawn: light is the masculine principle which heralds the dawn of patriarchal culture and the defeat of matriarchy. This defeat is accomplished by the forcible and final separation of Mildred and Veda, thus making it possible for Mildred to live with Bert in a 'normal' couple relationship. She is returned to point zero, completely stripped, rehabilitated. To understand why such violent repression had to be seen to be necessary it is important to look at the use of melodrama in the film.

Melodrama

The melodramatic sections of the film are set in the past, Mildred's own account of her history in terms of her rejection of her class (represented by Bert, who is critical of Mildred's petit-bourgeois aspirations, but is down on his luck, unemployed, his masculinity impaired) and her rejection of the patriarchal symbolic order (she expels Bert from the family and rejects Wally Fay as a substitute, taking over the place of father/provider herself). The crucial question posed at this point is, of course, 'Has Mildred the right to rule the family?' At first the answer seems to be positive, she is strong, hard-working, honest and single-minded, not to mention ambitious. She seems to possess precisely those characteristics lacking in the men. Mildred attempts to return to the Demetrian stage of matriarchy in which women command home and state, represented here by her family and her restaurant business. However, her retreat from patriarchy leads 'inevitably' through the cause and effect of narrative to the primitive stage of hetaerism and the deterioration of all social order, represented by Veda and Monty, whose relationship implies the Dionysian stage characterised by Bachofen as heralding the coming of patriarchy.

The first sign of deterioration comes when Mildred's one night of illicit passion with Monty is followed by Kay's death. The loss of one daughter strengthens Mildred's obsession with Veda, and with making a success of her business, in the course of which she forms a relationship of mutual solidarity with her friend Ida who helps her to run the business, while men (Wally and Monty) are relegated to the secondary status of instruments.

In the second flashback deterioration sets in, revolving around Veda's problem with finding a sexual identity, since she has no father, and a mother who is also a father. Sexual ambiguity is compounded by Veda's sexual blackmail of the Forrester family (aided by Wally), and the implication of a sexual relationship between Veda and Monty. Veda and Mildred separate after a confrontation, but Mildred cannot live without Veda, and finally marries Monty in order to get her back. While Veda and Monty enjoy themselves at a party, Mildred discovers that she has lost her business because Monty and Wally have done a deal without telling her. When she discovers that Veda and Monty have gone to the beach house together she follows them with the gun. At this point Mildred confesses to the murder of Monty.

Mildred's take-over of the place of the father has brought about the collapse of all social and moral order in her world: Monty and Veda are on the point of breaking the ultimate taboo: that against father incest. In the face of impending chaos and confusion the patriarchal order is called upon to reassert itself and take the Law back into its own hands, divesting women completely of any power they may have gained while the patriarchal order was temporarily impaired. This involves establishing the truth without a doubt, restoring 'normal' sexual relationships and reconstituting the family unit, in spite of the pain and suffering which such repressive action must cause. Pain and suffering are a necessary part of the work of reconstruction

The active mother in melodrama.

The active mother in film noir.

(represented by Bert, who has earned his right to take the place of the father again through suffering and self-sacrifice).

The split between melodrama/film noir is overcome by the force of the Law, and Bert and Mildred walk into the dawn together, reconstituted as a couple, the image bearing the marks of repression in the form of another couple from the past: two women who work together, this time to support the patriarchal institution by scrubbing the steps of the police station. They remain as a reminder of the consequences which would ensue should 'illicit' or ambiguous couplings become a possibility again.

The 'snare'

Barthes has emphasised the importance of *delay* to the unfolding of narrative.[8] In *S/Z* he isolates several forms of 'reticence' which are used to hold back the resolution of the enigma. The 'snare' is identified as a deliberate evasion of the Truth.

The act of involvement in 'classic' narrative is for the reader/viewer an act based on misrecognition. The reader suspends knowledge of the Truth for the required length of time: 'I know, but . . .' Pleasure is generated by the possibility of the return of infantile wishes and phantasies repressed by the passing through the Oedipus complex. In the 'classic' narrative knowledge is suspended for a limited amount of time and Truth is re-established at the end through the resolution of the enigma: thus 'classic' narrative re-enacts the Oedipal drama itself: the passage from misrecognition (the pre-Oedipal stage of bi-sexuality when both male and female are thought to possess a penis and the mother is the love-object of both male and female children) to knowledge (the discovery of the fact of castration through sight of the mother's body without a penis, at which point boys must identify with the father, who has the power of castration, and give up (temporarily) their desire for the mother, and girls must identify with the mother in her (already) castrated state, also giving up their desire for her. Thus boys and girls becôme 'sexed' human beings, relinquishing bi-sexuality in favour of the choice of a love-object from the opposite sex). 'Classic' narrative affirms this heterosexual structure. the mainstay of the family unit and of social reproduction, again and again.

Bachofen's description of the transition from mother-right to father-right corresponds in many ways to Freud's Oedipus complex, since the transition rests on the suppression of motherhood and the constant struggle of patriarchy to resist the return of an earlier matriarchal symbolic order characterised by greater sexual freedom and democracy.

In *Mildred Pierce* the Oedipal drama is re-enacted in an explicitly repressive form, since the 'snare', the deliberate withholding of the reverse-shot, which is the basis for the audience's 'misrecognition' of Mildred as an agent of death, is reinforced on several levels in the film, and the knowledge that Mildred is not the murderer is withheld from the viewer, so that the resolution of the enigma, the progress to 'knowledge', rests entirely with the detective as the representative of the Law.

As Monty dies, whispering 'Mildred', the next shot shows a car drawing away from the beach-house, in long-shot so that we cannot see who is driving. A dissolve leads us into a shot of Mildred walking on the pier in a suicidal state. Film noir lighting suggests duplicity: an unknown threat which might emerge from the shadows. Joan Crawford, who plays Mildred, is an ambiguous sexual figure as a star with a history of playing 'independent women' roles, emphasised in this scene by the broad shoulders of her coat. The fundamental misrecognition has been established as we are led to believe that Mildred is the murderer, that she has exercised the power of life and death which only the Father holds.

The 'snare' is compounded further when, in the following sequence, Mildred attempts to set Wally up for the murder, since we assume from what we 'know' so far that she is protecting herself from discovery. It is probable that she is the uncastrated mother, and the spectator is invited to enter into a pre-Oedipal phantasy, a recollection of a repressed, but not forgotten, time when much more sexual freedom was possible. At the same time, the phantasy is represented as increasingly threatening, encouraging the spectator to take up a defensive position and to wish for the resolution of ambiguity, to put an end to feelings of anxiety.[9]

The function of the first flashback is to articulate the phantasy by re-creating the circumstances in which Mildred denies her own castration by taking over as head of the family, and building up her own business. She invades the territory of men: that of property and investment, and after Kay's death rejects men as sexual partners, becoming obsessed with Veda and her work. Her relationship with Veda,[10] coupled with her close friendship with Ida (played by Eve Arden, another actress who is an ambiguous sexual figure), represents an attempt to return to the pre-Oedipal bisexual state, a regression from patriarchy. This regression includes the men too, who are represented as weak and dissipated, untrustworthy, except for Bert, who grows to maturity during the film.

Veda represents the consequences of this retreat from patriarchy. Her close physical resemblance to Mildred emphasises her function as a 'double', created by Mildred as a defence against castration.[11] She is, however, all the things that Mildred is not: deceitful, promiscuous, greedy and hysterical; she represents the threat of chaos, the excess which Mildred's discourse calls into being and which it cannot resolve.

The threat of chaos extends to the world of business as well. The evasion of the patriarchal law produces a situation in which nothing is stable, since business relationships are closely tied to sexual relationships in the film, and Mildred's business rests on the goodwill of her two partners, Wally and Monty, both less than reliable. These are hardly the best circumstances in which to rebuild an economy; in order to create a stable economic situation suitable for investment, sexual order must be re-established, excess and ambiguity must be resolved through a 'necessary' repression.

In her false confession Mildred claims to have resolved the excess herself by killing Monty. As I have already suggested, however, if Mildred had killed

Monty this would perpetuate the situation in which the mother is seen to have the power of life and death, in this case explicitly the power to enforce the taboo against incest. The situation of unresolved excess would remain, since Veda would go free.

The resolution of excess is achieved when the detective invalidates Mildred's confession, revealing that he knew the true murderer all the time. The existence of the 'snare' is made explicit, thus putting Mildred *and* the audience in the same position, at the mercy of the Law.* The resolution is articulated by the scene in which Veda confesses, believing that Mildred has betrayed her, and mother and daughter are separated for ever – Veda, the representative of excess, being removed for imprisonment or death. The final flashback, the 'true' story of the murder, confirms the resolution: when Mildred comes to the point of killing Monty she is incapable of doing so. Veda, however, is not, and kills Monty (surrogate father) in a frenzy of libidinal excess. The final flashback is shot in 'classic' noir style: it is not until Mildred and Bert are finally reunited under the aegis of the Law that ambiguity is resolved and the shadows dispersed by the light of the new day.

The body of the film[12]

i have tried to show that the problematic articulated by the film *Mildred Pierce* is one of uncertainty and duplicity, centred on Mildred's body as the location of sexual ambiguity, and the return of an infantile phantasy about the body of the mother, a phantasy which allows for a potentially more democratic structure of sexual relationships based on bisexuality, a structure repressed by the heterosexual division which the Oedipus complex attempts to enforce. The problematic is signified on one level by the relationship between Veda and Mildred: Veda is seen as a part of Mildred's body, an extension of herself, the phallus she will not relinquish. 'Veda is a part of me', Mildred says to Ida at one point, and publicity photographs of the film inevitably show Mildred holding Veda (and sometimes Kay as well) close to her.

I have tried to indicate that this phantasy of the mother's body, with its connotations of sexual excess and the erosion of the patriarchal order cannot be tolerated by the film, and is resolved by a brutal act of repression in which Mildred is castrated, not only through the invalidation of her discourse, but by her enforced separation from Veda (which allows for no possibility of emotional reconciliation) which amounts to an act of mutilation perpetrated by the police on Mildred's body.

I should like to suggest some ways in which I think an analogy is drawn between the 'body' of the film, its material structure, and Mildred's body as the location of duplicity.

* When the 'snare' is made explicit, the meaning of Monty's dying whisper, 'Mildred . . .', changes: Mildred now becomes the 'lost object', relegated to the past, a memory (cf., 'Rosebud' in *Citizen Kane*), rather than the agent of death.

Mildred as the location of duplicity.

Veda: the sign of excess.

The 'snare' utilised in the opening section serves a double function: it omits something (a reverse-shot), and then proceeds to mask the omission by the use of a long-shot of the car driving off, and a dissolve to Mildred on the pier. There is an absence, or lack, in the film which the film itself masks in the same way as Mildred masks her own 'lack'.

Masking also takes place on the level of *mise en scène*, in the use of film noir conventions of lighting: sharp contrasts of light and shadow suggest partial truth; something is missing, but whatever it is remains hidden. Since the enjoyment of the phantasy rests on the temporary masking of the truth, the insertion of the film noir segments into the structure of the film both reinforces the phantasy and reminds the spectator that something is to be revealed.

The use of even lighting and more classic shot compositions in Mildred's discourse indicate a plenitude, a situation in which nothing is missing and which belongs to the past, as the mother's body represented plenitude for the child in the pre-Oedipal situation. Again, the interruptions by the film noir segments serve both to confirm the ambiguity upon which the phantasy of plenitude is based, and to remind us that something is hidden. The presence of two markedly different styles of film genre underlines the sexual ambiguity in the structure of the film itself, since each genre is specifically associated with a different audience and market: melodrama with women and film noir with men.

What is hidden in the body of the film is eventually revealed as the presence of the father as agent of the Law, represented by the detective, who was actually in control of the structure of the film all the time, who unmasks the gap and then proceeds to fill it with the missing reverse-shot, thus revealing the 'lack' in the mother's body (the body of the film), into which he inserts his own discourse, the Truth. The enigma is resolved by dispelling ambiguity in favour of patriarchy and a symbolic order based on heterosexuality which it implies, explicitly suppressing matriarchy and reconstituting Bert and Mildred as a 'normal' heterosexual couple.

As Mildred and Bert walk off into the light of the new dawn from which all shadow and duplicity has been erased, they turn their backs on another couple, two women in the classic position of oppression, on their knees: an image of sacrifice which closes the film with a reminder of what women must give up for the sake of the patriarchal order.[13]

Notes

1. See, for instance, Stephen Farber, 'Violence and the Bitch Goddess', *Film Comment*, Nov/Dec 1974; and John Davis, 'The Tragedy of Mildred Pierce', *Velvet Light Trap*, No. 6.
2. Described in J.A. Place and L.S. Peterson, 'Some Visual Motifs of Film Noir'. *Film Comment*, Jan 1974, and Paul Schrader, 'Notes on Film Noir', *Film Comment*, Spring 1972.
3. J.J. Bachofen, *Myth, Religion and Mother Right:* selected writings, 1861; Princeton University Press/Bollingen Foundation, New Jersey, 1973.

4. See, for instance, Frederick Engels in *The Origin of the Family, Private Property, and the State*, 1884; Pathfinder Press, New York, 1973.

5. James Cain's novel *Mildred Pierce*, which appeared in 1941, is significantly different from the film in that it presents Mildred's story in terms of her economic, emotional and sexual problems after the break-up of her marriage to Bert. The film draws more on myth and less on naturalistic detail than the novel.

6. Joyce Nelson, *'Mildred Pierce* Reconsidered', *Film Reader*, No. 2.

7. Interesting attempts to define melodrama in terms of excess have been made by Laura Mulvey in 'Notes on Sirk and Melodrama', *Movie*, No. 25, and by Geoffrey Nowell-Smith in 'Minnelli and Melodrama', *Screen*, v18 n2.

8. Roland Barthes, 'Delay', *S/Z*, Jonathan Cape, London 1975, p.75.

9. Anxiety feelings similar to those which cause us to wake up when a dream threatens to go beyond the pleasure principle. The detective's action in opening the blinds could be interpreted as a metaphor for waking up.

10. In the novel, Mildred's relationship with Veda is represented as explicitly sexual, in the physical and emotional sense.

11. The relationship of physical similarity between Mildred and Veda represents in Freudian terms Mildred's choice of a love object based on narcissism, the dyadic relationship which the Oedipus complex attempts to resolve. The 'wicked' side of Veda seems to represent the underside of Demetrian matriarchy, the unregulated excesses of hetaerism.

12. Two articles which discuss the concept of film as 'body' are 'Minnelli and Melodrama' (see above) and Mark Nash, 'Notes on the Dreyer-text', *Dreyer*, BFI, London 1977.

13. It is worth noting that Bachofen associates the number 2 with the feminine principle of justice in the section on Egypt in *Myth, Religion, and Mother Right* (see above). The two women on the steps of the police station could be said to represent the subjugation of matriarchal Law.

The place of women in Fritz Lang's
The Blue Gardenia

E. Ann Kaplan

In the typical film noir, the world is presented from the point of view of the male investigator, who often recounts something that happened in the past. The investigator, functioning in a nightmare world where all the clues to meaning are deliberately hidden, seeks to unravel a mystery with which he has been presented. He is in general a reassuring presence in the noir world: we identify with him and rely on him to use reason and cunning, if not to outwit the criminals then at least to solve the enigma.

By contrast, the female characters in film noir stand outside the male order and represent a challenge to it.[1] They symbolise all that is evil and mysterious. Sexuality being the only weapon women have in relation to men, they use it to entrap the investigator and prevent him from accomplishing his task. Dangerous because their sexuality is so openly displayed and so irresistible, women become the element that the male investigator must guard against if he is to succeed in his quest.

The Blue Gardenia is a challenge to critics,[2] because in it Lang does not simply follow noir conventions in the manner that he does in two other films (*The Big Heat* and *Human Desire*) made about the same time. Lang rather turns noir conventions upside down in *The Blue Gardenia* by presenting two separate discourses – that is, two modes of articulating a vision of reality.[3] There is the usual male discourse familiar from noir films and represented here by Casey Mayo, journalist playing investigator, and the police; but alongside this, Lang has inserted the discourse of Norah, a young telephone operator – a discourse that presents the confusion and alienation of women in a male world. As I'll show, Lang's treatment of Norah exposes male assumptions about women in noir films; by juxtaposing the male discourse, with its noir conventions, to Norah's point of view, Lang reveals elements of that discourse that generally go unquestioned.[4]

The film opens in an apparently traditional manner, with Mayo driving up to the West Coast Telephone Company and leaving his sleepy photographer in the car. Inside, we find Prebble flirting with Crystal, a friend who lives with Norah and who is also a telephone operator. Prebble, called to the phone, is irritated with demands being made by an hysterical woman. Visually, the men dominate the frames in the expected manner. Prebble is shot lounging beside Crystal, sitting above her and facing the camera. Mayo dominates by standing up and both men act seductively to the women, Mayo in a less sinister and offensive way than Prebble.

The second scene, set in the apartment that Crystal, Norah and Sally share, is in striking contrast to the first. The female discourse is now evident, although the women are still placed symbolically in a subordinate way to men. The cosy relationships among the working women and the sense of a female world recall Arzner's films and other so-called 'women's films', like LaCava's *Stagedoor* and Bacon's *Marked Woman*. Visually, the women occupy the centre of the frames and face the camera. Within the privacy of their home, they have more confident gestures and body postures, and freely extend themselves in the space they are in as was not possible when men were *physically* present. There is friendly repartee between the women and obvious support and caring for each other.

But, as in the 'women's films' mentioned, the symbolic importance of men assures their domination even when absent. Men provide the main topic of interest and although presented from the women's point of view, their centrality to the women's lives is clear. Each woman has made her own accommodation to the need to have a man: Sally finds real men boring, and lives a vicarious but passionate love life through pulp fiction; Crystal is dating her ex-husband, Homer, having discovered that she gets much more out of the relationship this way; Norah at the beginning of the scene is in love with her soldier in Korea, and lives for his return.

Norah's sudden discovery of her soldier's infidelity sets the narrative in motion and conditions her behaviour on the fatal night of Prebble's murder. Earlier on in the evening, her friends had ridiculed Norah for preferring a lonely birthday supper with her fiance's photograph to a night out. Anticipating that the letter she has saved for this moment will be full of his love for her, Norah is cruelly disappointed by an abrupt announcement of the soldier's imminent wedding to a nurse. At this point, Prebble telephones for a date with Crystal, whose number he had finally obtained earlier in the day. Pretending to be Crystal, Norah accepts the date herself, out of a desperate need to drown her hurt.

Taken aback at first to see Norah instead of Crystal, Prebble quickly adjusts to the situation, the implication being that the particular girl does not matter that much to him. He sees that Norah gets thoroughly drunk at the Blue Gardenia club, where Cole Porter sings the Gardenia song and a blind woman sells gardenia flowers. He then takes Norah back to his apartment where he begins to make love to her. Norah goes drunkenly along at first, pretending her lover is her fiance, but on realising her mistake, she wants to leave. Prebble insists, and in defence against being raped, Norah grabs a poker and strikes out at him, fainting before she can see what she has done. Waking up some time later, she rushes out of the house without her shoes, and goes home.

When Norah gets up the next morning, she has no memory of the events that took place in Prebble's apartment. While on the level of the surface narrative, this is a clumsy device for providing the enigma that has to be solved, it has symbolic importance in relation to the placing of women. Norah's inability to 'remember' or to say what actually happened represents the common experience of women in patriarchy — that of feeling unable to reason well because the terms in which the culture thinks are male and alien. Women in patriarchy do not function competently at the level of external, public articulation, and thus may appear 'stupid' and 'uncertain'.[5] Norah's 'forgetting' dramatically symbolises her lostness in the male noir world of the film; she experiences a nightmare-like feeling of not knowing whether she is innocent or guilty, and of being therefore vulnerable to male manipulation.

The *mise en scène* of the opening sequences underscores Norah's vulnerability; the male world is presented visually as a labyrinth through which she cannot find her way and which is fraught with danger for her. There is a dramatic contrast between the *mise en scène* in scenes representing the women's worlds (the telephone company, the women's apartment), and that in the male worlds (The Blue Gardenia Club, Prebble's apartment, and, later on, Mayo's office). While the scenes in the telephone company and the apartment are brightly lit, the atmosphere cheerful and bustling, those in the male locations are shot in noir style, with looming shadows, unusual camera angles, objects awkwardly placed in the frame, etc., to create a sinister, claustrophobic atmosphere.[6] The first scene in the women's apartment demonstrates the threatening aspect of the male world for Norah in the dramatic change that takes place once the other women have left, and Norah discovers her soldier's betrayal.

Even before we know this, however, Lang has prepared us for something unpleasant. Norah is dressed in a black taffeta dress, and has darkened the room, supposedly to create a romantic candle-lit, atmosphere, but as she sits down the shadows loom ominously. She sits opposite her fiance's picture almost as if before an icon, the candle-light adding to the sense of something unnatural going on. Lang seems to be deliberately exposing the excessive nature of Norah's devotion here, as if to increase the shock of the soldier's infidelity. Once his voice is heard, Norah translating the letter to her lover's spoken speech, the scene becomes even more sinister and ominous, the shadows darkening to the point of seeming almost to invade the light. When the phone rings, and Norah crosses the room to answer it, the music becomes sinister and the screen is almost black.

The women's apartment, thus, is seen to change dramatically, to become sinister and threatening, once men symbolically invade it. The Blue Gardenia Club next presents the male world as manipulative, seeking to trap unaware women. We first see Prebble at the Club setting up his seduction and making jokes about women with Mayo, who is at the bar on the pick-up. As Norah enters, she is seen in long shot, a tiny figure lost in the maze of the elaborate

The Blue Gardenia

Hawaiian decor of the Club. Guided to Prebble's secluded table, she is seated in a wicker chair with an enormous back that seems to swallow her up. Things become more sinister again as the couple drive home in the pouring rain and thunderstorm. The shots of the car hood closing over the couple suggest that Norah is being trapped, as does the corresponding shot of the skylight window in Prebble's apartment with the rain beating down on it from the outside. Once the couple move into the living room, the *mise en scène* becomes even more sinister; there is a large mirror on the wall, surrounded by plants that cast eerie shadows over the room. It is as if Norah is lost in a jungle, the decor symbolising male traps and wiles.

It is important to note that it is only at this point that Prebble begins to appear in a sinister light. The section of the film up to this point has merely presented the alternating discourses of the men, on the one hand, and Norah (and to a degree the other women) on the other, both being shown as equally 'valid'. As the film goes on, however, and as we come to identify increasingly with Norah rather than the men, so the male discourse begins to be undercut by that of Norah. Reversing the situation in most noir films, where women are seen only within the male discourse, here that discourse is demystified through the fact that Norah is allowed to present herself directly to us. There are three main ways in which the male discourse is challenged.

The first way in which the male discourse is undercut is through Norah's knowing more than the male investigators about what went on the night of the murder. As already noted, in most noir films we identify with the male investigator and rely on him to bring at least some coherence in an essentially chaotic world. Here, however, we identify with Norah and have been present, as Mayo and the police have not, in Prebble's apartment the night of the murder. Although neither we nor Norah know all the facts, we at least know that she was the girl in Prebble's room who left her shoes and handkerchief there, and who was wearing a taffeta dress. On the evidence we have, it seems likely that Norah did kill Prebble in self-defence, but we are sympathetic to her hesitation in giving herself up to the police. Because we are seeing from Norah's point of view, we identify with her, not the investigators, whom we perceive from the outside trying to piece together parts of a puzzle that already fit for us.

A second way in which the male discourse is undercut is through the perspective we acquire, by being placed in Norah's consciousness, on the hypotheses that Mayo and the police develop about the woman who was with Prebble on the.night of the murder. They automatically assume that she was no good (most likely a prostitute, since what decent woman would go out with Prebble), and that she deserves all she will get for murdering Prebble. (There is, however, no condemnation of Prebble's seductions, no suggestion that he may have exploited women for his own ends, or taken advantage of women's loneliness.) The disjunction between Norah, whom we experience as a gentle, warm and honest person, and the 'fictional' woman the men and society in general conjure up, highlights the harsh stereotype that women must deal with and the sexual double standard.

Particularly painful for Norah is the way even her close friends assume that the woman with Prebble was no good, and is to be despised and punished. Through the device of Norah's increasing identification with the heroines of Sally's pulp fiction, Lang notes Norah's growing self-hatred as she hears the comments about the 'Prebble woman'. Earlier on, Sally discussed with zest her latest book about a 'red debutante [who] is hit on the head, stabbed in the back, and shot in the stomach'. Norah's increasing identification with these pulp fiction women is made clear after an upsetting conversation with Sally and Crystal about the murderess. When the two friends leave Norah in the kitchen, she picks up a knife and holds it suggestively toward her stomach. We cut to a cover of one of Sally's books, showing a woman brandishing a knife with a terrible grimace on her face; the image echoes Norah's growing frustration as she feels condemned, trapped and helpless.

Norah's increasing sense of being trapped comes from her inability to withstand a definition of herself imposed by an alien and indecipherable male discourse. She does not trust her own sense of what she is, or is not, capable of, uncertain as to where male definitions end and her own begin. As the events of her night with Prebble are reconstructed for her by the police, Norah suffers a terrifying dislocation from reality. Not having evidence to the contrary, she comes to accept their definition of her as a murderess, despite an underlying sense that something is amiss. She is reduced to a state of hysteria, acting like a criminal, jumping when she sees the police, burning evidence like the taffeta dress, listening secretly to the radio in the dead of night. Her personality changes, and she becomes irritable with her friends. She thus folds up under the weight of the male structuring of things, succumbs to their view of her, and takes the guilt upon herself.

The third way in which the male discourse is undercut is through the perspective we develop on Casey Mayo. Identified as we are with Norah, the alternation between the discourses 'places' what Mayo is doing and allows us to see it for what it is. In the ordinary noir film, the investigator's trapping of the murderess would be a demonstration of his triumph over sexuality and evil. Here, Mayo is seen to engineer a despicable betrayal of the murderess whose dilemma he exploits for a publicity stunt. He pretends to be the killer's friend, seductively offering help and secrecy but all along intending to give the girl up to the police once she has revealed herself to him. Norah resists Mayo's appeals for a long time (while, by the way, the audience is 'entertained' by a series of false responses by desperate women, who are made ridiculous), but her isolation finally wears her down. She is unable to confide in her women friends (although we sense that at least Crystal would be sympathetic), partly because they have spoken so badly of the Prebble 'woman', but also because Norah presumably does not see them as being able to help. She assumes that only men, those in the place of power, can get her out of her fix. She thus turns to Casey Mayo, who has been presenting himself over the radio as someone able to make reason out of chaos.

Because of the total trust with which Norah turns to Mayo, his treatment of her is shocking. When she comes to him posing as the murderess' friend,

Mayo responds warmly to her, partly because he is attracted to her but also because he is anxious to be the first to discover the murderess. When Norah finally reveals that she is herself the supposed murderess, Mayo's response is terrifying: she is now repulsive to him, someone to be shunned, cast off. He does not quite decide to turn her in himself as originally planned — because of his attraction — but is glad to be sent off on another job.

Lang's visual treatment of the meeting between Mayo and Norah underscores her vulnerability, and Mayo's manipulation. He asks Norah to meet him late at night in his office. Norah's arrival is shot from Mayo's point of view: when he hears the elevator coming, he shuts off the lights, presumably so that he will be able to size her up before she has a chance to see him. Also, perhaps, to frighten her. We see Norah emerge from the lit elevator in the back of the frame; she is a tiny figure in black, in the lit corridor, with the threatening blackness of Mayo's office looming in front of her. Mayo watches silently as she slowly makes her way up the dark room, lit only from outside. The visual presentation of the scene expresses Mayo's power over Norah, her dependence on him and his unworthiness to be trusted, since he thinks only in terms of power and not of human vulnerability. Mayo is exposed as incapable of pity or empathy, and as bound by stereotypes of women as either 'good' or 'bad' girls.

The progressive elements of *The Blue Gardenia* that I've been discussing are, as so often, undercut by the way the film ends. Mayo has to be 'redeemed' by being the one who finally *does* solve the mystery of who murdered Prebble. By noticing a discrepancy between the record Norah said was on the phonograph at the time of the murder and that found by the police on the turntable when they arrived, Mayo tracks the murderess down; she turns out to be the hysterical woman Prebble had rejected at the start of the film. Mayo's reward for liberating Norah is of course to win her for himself; he now has the 'good' woman and can throw over his black book to his delighted photographer.

Although by the end of the film all the structures defining men and women are safely back in place, Lang's achievement remains. In turning noir conventions upside down, *The Blue Gardenia* has revealed the place that women usually occupy in these films. We see that the view men have of women is false in that the set of implications about Norah generated from the male world turn out to be invalid. While the male discourse tried to define Norah as a *femme fatale*, we see rather that she is a victim of male strategies to ensnare her for something she did not do. Norah's submissive placing of herself in relation to the male world is also exposed. She accepts the male view of her and then experiences the world as a riddle that she cannot solve. In this way, *The Blue Gardenia* exposes the essential contradiction between the dominant male discourse and the subordinate (repressed) discourse of women in patriarchy.

Notes

1. Relevant here is the statement that Laura Mulvey makes in *The Riddles of the Sphinx* in the second section where she is reading directly into the camera. Looking to the world of mythology for an understanding of women's place in patriarchy, Mulvey describes the Sphinx as representing the unconscious and women. Mulvey says:

   > The Sphinx is outside the city gates, she challenges the culture of the city, with its order of kinship and its order of knowledge, a culture and a political system which assign women a subordinate place.
   >
   > '*Riddles of the Sphinx:* A film by Laura Mulvey and Peter Wollen', *Screen* v18 n2, Summer 1977, p62.

   Women in film noir in particular are placed in the position of the Sphinx. mysterious. sinister and challenging to men but assigned a place outside the order of the film.

2. There has been little extended treatment of *The Blue Gardenia*, and the film has in the main been dismissed as a poor example of Lang's work. Paul Jensen, for instance, says that Lang's 'rejection of the narrative qualities of mystery and suspense is so complete that it must be intentional', concluding that 'the film's sole distinction remains its introduction of the theme song'. In *Fritz Lang*, New York 1969, p181.

3. I am using the notion of 'discourse' as developed firstly by Colin MacCabe in 'Realism and the Cinema: Notes on some Brechtian Themes'. *Screen*, v15 n2, Summer 1974, pp7-27, and later on by Claire Johnston and Pam Cook in *The Work of Dorothy Arzner*, British Film Institute, London 1975. Its use here is similar also to that of Pam Pam Cook in her piece on *Mildred Pierce*, also included in this volume.

4. This is not the first time that Lang has worked in a 'progressive' (cf., MacCabe) manner in a classic text. Noel Burch's analysis of *M* ('De *Mabuse* a *M*: Le travail de Fritz Lang', in *Revue D'Esthétique*, numéro spécial, 1973) shows how Lang used techniques to distance viewers in order to present an extraordinarily complex image of the child murderer and the society he lived in. According to Burch, Lang abandons literary conceptions of character and narrative, and works rather through '*la langage sans langue*' that Metz calls cinema. In an unpublished dissertation on Lang, Julian Petley notes that in *The Return of Frank James*, Lang seems interested in exploring the processes in the Western genre by which the outlaw becomes a hero, rather than in simply presenting the hero without question, *The Films of Fritz Lang: The Cinema as Destiny*, unpublished thesis, Exeter 1973, p22.

5. Here again Mulvey's words in *Riddles* illuminate the point usefully. If women in traditional film noir are in the Sphinx position, in Lang's film what Mulvey has to say about women within patriarchy applies:

   > To the patriarchy, the Sphinx as woman is a threat and a riddle, but women within patriarchy are faced with a neverending series of threats and riddles – dilemmas which are hard for women to solve, because the culture within which they must think is not theirs. We live in a society ruled by the father, in which the place of the mother is suppressed. . . And meanwhile the Sphinx can only speak with a voice apart, a voice off. (p62)

6. In Pam Cook's 'Duplicity in *Mildred Pierce*', she notes a similar contrast between the flashback sequences, that have to do with Mildred's subject matter – the family, sexual and emotional relationships, work, property and investment and the noir parts of the film related to men. Mildred's story, Cook says, is the 'stuff of which the "Woman's Picture" was made . . .' The style here is different from that in the rest of the film, scenes being 'evenly lit, few variations of camera angle, etc.' In contrast the framing noir discourse is marked by classic noir style. She concludes that there are two voices, female and male within the film, each roughly corresponding to the Woman's picture and the Man's film and with its own style. The divisions interestingly enough roughly correspond to those I've noted in *The Blue Gardenia* between Norah's discourse and that of the male, noir discourse, also filmed in classic noir style.

Resistance through charisma:
Rita Hayworth and *Gilda*

Richard Dyer

The argument of this article is that in *Gilda* it is possible to read the generic construction of Gilda as *femme fatale* as being in some measure overturned and exposed, partly by certain features of *mise en scène*, partly by the casting of Rita Hayworth in the part. The argument is based on three assumptions: about film noir, about stars, and about critical reading.

Film noir

Apart from certain broadly generic features (e.g., labyrinthine narrative structures, 'expressionist' lighting and composition, an iconography of hard-boiled heroes, *femmes fatales* and decadence, etc.), film noir is characterised by a certain anxiety over the existence and definition of masculinity and normality. This anxiety is seldom directly expressed and yet may be taken to constitute the films' 'problematic', that set of issues and questions that the films seek to come to terms with without ever actually articulating. (To articulate them would already be to confront masculinity and normality as problems, whereas ideology functions on the assumption that they can be taken for granted.) This problematic can be observed in, on the one hand, the films' difficulty in constructing a positive image of masculinity and normality, which would constitute a direct assertion of their existence and definition, and, on the other hand, the films' use of images of that which is *not* masculine and normal – i.e., that which is feminine and deviant – to mark off the parameters of the categories that they are unable actually to show.

To illustrate this. The heroes of film noir are for the most part either colourless characterisations (cf., the parade of anodyne performers in the central roles – Dana Andrews, Glenn Ford, Farley Granger) and/or characters conspicuously lacking in the virtues of the 'normal' man (e.g., John Garfield, immigrant, loner, a red; Fred MacMurray as a weak insurance sales-man in *Double Indemnity*; Ralph Meeker, plain nasty and unattractive). The exceptions are the characters played by Humphrey Bogart and Robert Mitchum, and it would be interesting to analyse whether it is these characters as written or only as played that makes them seem to be positive assertions of masculine norms. The fact that most film noir heroes are rootless and unmarried, and the implication of quasi-gay relationships in certain instances (*Dead Reckoning, The Big Combo, Double Indemnity, Gilda,* inter alia), all serve to rob them, as they are substantially constructed, of the attributes of masculinity and normality. Consequently the burden for assuring us of the continued validity of these traditional notions falls to other elements of character and milieu construction in the films.

There are two aspects to this. First, film noir abounds in colourful representations of decadence, perversion, aberration etc. Such characters and milieux vividly evoke that which is not normal, through connotations (including of femininity, homosexuality and art) of that which is not masculine. By inference the hero, questing his way through these characters and milieux, is normal and masculine.

Secondly, women in film noir are above all else unknowable. It is not so much their evil as their unknowability (and attractiveness) that makes them fatal for the hero. To the degree that culture is defined by men, what is, and is known, is male. Film noir thus starkly divides the world into that which is unknown and unknowable (female) and, again by inference only, that which is known (male).

In this context, any film noir that allows us to 'know' the *femme fatale*, not in the way the hero comes to know her (i.e., by having knowledge of her, finally controlling her), but in the way we 'know' all major characters in novelistic fiction, is making trouble for itself. Once the woman is not the eternal unknowable, the hitherto concealed inadequacy of the hero is liable to become evident. This is what happens in *Gilda*.

Stars
One of the central themes of Molly Haskell's *From Reverence to Rape* is the capacity of the great women stars to 'resist' the demeaning roles to which they were assigned. Haskell theorises this in terms of certain stars' 'sheer will and talent and determination'.[1] Whilst not wishing to diminish the real struggles over representation of women such as Mae West, Greta Garbo, Bette Davis and Marilyn Monroe, it might be more useful to think this in terms of the signifying function of a star's image within a film. A star's image is constructed both from her or his film appearances (typical roles, modes of presentation, performance and dress styles, etc.) and publicity (including promotion, advertising, fan magazines and gossip). In any particular film, this image is an already signifying complex of meaning and affect. The problem then arises of the 'fit' between this complex and the character the star plays as written and otherwise constructed (e.g., through dress, *mise en scène* etc.). In the case of *Gilda*, certain elements in Rita Hayworth's image do fit the generic *femme fatale*, but others do not, and this 'misfit' is sufficient to

foreground the functions of the *femme fatale* in relation to the problematic adequacy of the hero.

Critical reading

In the analysis of *Gilda* that follows, I am not aiming to produce a definitive reading, nor yet a 'counter-reading' in the spirit of 'semiotic guerrilla warfare'.[2] Rather, I am interested in indicating some of the readings that the film makes possible. In this case, the readings are in certain respects mutually contradictory, and this suggests something of the terrain of ideological struggle within which the film is situated. In this respect these readings need to be returned to the specificities of the film's audiences (e.g., its contemporary cinema audiences, old-movies-on-television audiences, readers-of-articles-like-this audiences etc.) – something we have not yet learnt how to do.

Gilda

Johnny

Through the decisive device of the voice-over, *Gilda* is very much signalled as being Johnny/Glenn Ford's film. It is his story, his point-of-view, his destiny that is to concern us. He has the double quest of the film noir – to solve the mystery of the villain and of the woman – and his voice-over guides us through it. Within this, we are repeatedly told what to think of Gilda, to side with him in his denunciation of her, to rejoice in his final possession of her.

Equally, there is no question but that Gilda/Hayworth is set up as another *femme fatale* in the film noir tradition. She is the object of desire in a type of film in which the object of desire is unknowable and treacherous. Hayworth's successful previous roles in dramas (as opposed to her roles in musicals) were as the 'other woman' (*Only Angels Have Wings, Strawberry Blonde*) and most vividly as an archetypal evil seductress in *Blood and Sand*, roles that made it easy to read Gilda in *femme fatale* terms. She is moreover dressed in the film with that combination of artifice and sensuality characteristic of the noir woman (cf., especially the use of long hair, coiffed to appear naturally 'unreally' lustrous and flowing, and of tactile fabrics like velvet and satin made into dresses that make obvious use of bones to distort the figure).

Yet compelling as these conventions are (the voice-over, the film type, the star image), it is not so easy either to identify with Johnny as the hero or to assent to his view of Gilda. This is partly because he is oddly placed in the film in relation to her and the other main character, Ballen, and partly because Gilda is Hayworth.

The problematic of masculinity and normality is particularly keen in *Gilda* by virtue of the implications of gayness that are built into the relationship between Johnny and Ballen. Apart from evidence external to the film,[3] the manner of Ballen's picking up Johnny, the exchanges of glances and the innuendoes of the dialogue between the two of them, all point to this dimension of their relationship.[4] More importantly, for the concerns of this article, Johnny, the hero of the film, is placed in the position of the woman within the relationship. (As is characteristic of filmic treatment of gays, the Ballen-Johnny relationship not only assumes such relationships are sick, decadent etc., but also assumes that they are structured according to the male-female norms of heterosexual relationships.) This is suggested from the very first scene in which Ballen picks him up. (He rescues him from a fight with some dice players and, taking a fancy to him, invites him to his casino where he becomes his right-hand man.) It becomes more explicit when Gilda arrives on the scene.

By a series of parallels, the significance of which Gilda, but not Johnny, is shown to be fully aware, the film shows Johnny to be placed in the same position *vis-a-vis* Ballen as Gilda is. They are both his pick-ups. Both say that they have no past, living only from the moment they met Ballen: 'I was down and out – he put me on my feet', says Johnny, to which Gilda replies, 'What a coincidence'. All this is explicable, if you follow the extremely elliptical dialogue very closely, in terms of Johnny and Gilda desiring to bury the past that contains their relationship to each other. This is, however, never clearly stated and what is said is also meant to be about their present common relationship to Ballen. Hayworth's glamour, a given of using her in the film at all, is complemented by a definite glamorisation of Ford. Where his previous appearances (mainly in westerns and other action films) use harsh lighting, close cropped hair and rough costuming, in *Gilda* he is softly lit (with his weakly sensual mouth in particular highlighted), his hair is brilliantined (thus rendered an interesting visual surface) and he is fastidiously dressed. In these respects then Ford-as-hero is none the less structurally placed and to a degree visually constructed as an object of desire.

If Johnny and Gilda are both objects of desire for Ballen and the camera, they are also objects of desire for each other. It is Gilda's traditional noir woman's function to be this, as well as Hayworth's. What is surprising about the film is the degree to which Johnny/Ford is in turn established as an object of her desire. In their first meeting in the film there is an exact reciprocity in the exchange of looks between Johnny and Gilda. From the moment we first see Gilda in this scene, cut in on a movement tossing her hair back and looking straight to where Johnny is standing, each shot of her looking at him is complemented by a shot of him looking at her. Each shot is of equal length; a shot over his shoulder matches a shot over hers, and so on; the sensuous play of light is identical. This establishment of him as an object of desire – which at the verbal level is also signalled as a desire she does not welcome – is maintained, though less forcibly, throughout the film, in the way he is photographed and in her repeated remarks on how 'pretty' he is.

In these ways, Johnny/Ford, despite his voice-over and status as protagonist, is placed in the position of the woman (in patriarchy), looking but also to be looked at. Once this is established, however, it seriously questions his authority as narrator, and in particular the degree to which we perceive Gilda through his judgement of her in voice-over. We are told that she is superstitious, that she is frightened, that she is promiscuous, but we see only the slenderest evidence of it (even accepting that conventions concerning promiscuity in 1946 were different from today). After their marriage, when she comes to beg him to be a husband to her, we are told by him (voice-over) that it is 'wonderful' — but by this stage in the film, it is questionable whether we are going to share this response to her evident humiliation. There is an increasing disjunction between Johnny as the signalled narrator and the actual narration of the plot and of Gilda.

Gilda

Although placed (by the role in this film type, by Hayworth's image, by the film's publicity) as the dangerous and unknowable function of the hero's destiny, this traditional placing of Gilda has been put at risk by the exceptional placing of Johnny/Ford in the film. This gives the character of Gilda the kind of illusion of 'autonomy' and 'being there for her own sake' (and not just for the sake of the hero) usually reserved for men in film. This is further achieved through giving Gilda a 'private' moment and through other elements in the Hayworth image.

Private moments, in the rhetoric of Hollywood character construction, are moments of truth. What they tell us about the character is privileged over what the character says (and even does) in public. The moment in question in *Gilda* is her first rendition of 'Put the Blame on Mame'. This is not strictly private. She sings it to the men's room attendant. However, his presence if anything reinforces the privileged quality of this moment, for he is signalled throughout the film as the wise man, down to earth, of the people, who 'understands' Gilda. Their relationship is constructed such that it assumes a transparency between them. Nor is the scene totally unobserved (within the film) — Johnny does come in on the end of it. However, it is sung in large part without his presence as observer, and the use of close-ups in the song powerfully asserts the truth of Gilda's expression at this moment. (Close-ups are one of the central mechanisms for the construction of the private.)

All this signalling as a moment of privileged access to Gilda's character is devoted to a song which points to how men always blame natural disasters on Mame — that is, women. The song states the case against the way film noir characteristically constructs women. The content of the song, together with its privileging *mise en scene*, points to the illegitimacy of men blaming women, where film noir generally is concerned to assert just that. (In *The Lady From Shanghai*, this rhetoric of the private is used to generate a certain pity for the Hayworth character, as it is here, but only all the more bitterly to expose by the end of the film this very appeal for pity as the *femme fatale*'s most damnable wile of all.)

This moment of truth informs the rest of the film. We are likely to use it to read Gilda's collapse at Johnny's feet (when the phoney lawyer brings her back to him from Buenos Aires) not with sadistic delight (as the voice-over urges us) but with pity or identification. The second, public rendition of 'Put the Blame on Mame' becomes a song of defiance, not just of a trapped wife against her husband, but of a woman against the male system.

The casting of Hayworth as Gilda gives the character a positive charge (where *femmes fatales* are usually negative, in the sense of being absent in terms of personality, mere functions or the eternal unknowable). This is, to begin with, partly due to the sheer status of Hayworth as a star. As one might expect from films that were usually low-budget productions, the *femmes fatales* of film noir were not usually played by major stars. (Crawford as Mildred Pierce belongs to the 'woman's film' emphasis of that film; only Barbara Stanwyck in *Double Indemnity* and Lana Turner in *The Postman Always Rings Twice* compare with Hayworth as major stars playing *femmes fatales*.) Hayworth was already established as a star with a known image and biography. In this sense, she has charisma. This is not in fact a 'magic presence', but it is constructed and experienced in this way. It is difficult for a *femme fatale* to be unknowable and 'absent', when incarnated by someone so known and present as Rita Hayworth. (Only by the most implacable destruction of Hayworth's image, including, crucially, cropping her hair and changing its colour, was Orson Welles able to do this in *The Lady From Shanghai*.)

It is not just her star status that gives Hayworth her presence in the film. It is also her position as an identification figure, and her dancing. Both of these relate to the issue of Hayworth as a sex object for the male viewer. The first raises the question of the female viewer, the second that of the processes of objectification.

Hayworth was primarily a 'love goddess', and as such very much a star for heterosexual men. However, by the time of *Gilda*, elements were accruing to the Hayworth image that would, in traditional terms, make her an identification figure for heterosexual women. These were partly her role as partner (rather than menace) in musicals, and partly details of her life surrounding marriage – married to a businessman in 1937, divorced 1942, married to Orson Welles 1943, bearing a daughter 1945 (just before shooting *Gilda*). What Gilda/Hayworth does can thus be read not only as a projection of male fantasy but also as an identification of female life concerns. (This is complicated. We do not know what audience members, female or male, do with films, in general or in specific instances, and women may identify with the most exotic of male projections. More importantly, the life concerns of marriage-and-family are very much to do with where women are placed within a male-dominated society. To say that women might identify with a star/character by virtue of the latter's involvement in marriage-and-family is only to acknowledge that many women are interested in the place to which they have been assigned.)

No other *femme fatale* dances. Undoubtedly the numbers in *Gilda* are there because Hayworth was known as a dancer, rather than for any necessity of the Gilda character. However, once there, they introduce a new element into the construction of the character as a sexual object – namely, movement.

It is worth noting first, that Hayworth dances in a manner different in certain respects from that of previous leading women dancers in Hollywood. Unlike Ginger Rogers, Hayworth did not require a partner for her dancing; and unlike Eleanor Powell, who did do solo numbers, Hayworth's style is not mechanical and virtuoso. (Powell is technically the most brilliant tap-dancer film star, but she does not use tap expressively.) The use of dance as 'self-expression' as instanced by Fred Astaire was also available to and used by Hayworth (though always in a less developed form than Astaire's). Although 'self-expression' is a problematic concept in relation to the arts, as a notion informing artistic practices, and especially dance, it is extremely important, and especially in the context of a character who is generically constructed as having no knowable self.

The comparison with Rogers and Powell is also important in terms of style. The former is identified principally with social dance (the Astaire-Rogers *pas de deux* are elaborations on the waltz, foxtrot etc.), and iconographically with social dance in the upper echelons of society. Powell, on the other hand, was billed as 'The World's Greatest Tap Dancer', a dance form associated principally in this period with the white appropriation of (black) tap dance in vaudeville. Hayworth, by contrast, dances in a Latin American style, and even if this were not recognisable from the dancing, it was known through her image (her parents were Spanish and she started work as a member of their Spanish dance troupe; Spain is not Latin America, but the popularity of Latin American dances in the forties made the slippage from one to the other easy, and *Gilda* compounds it by being set in South America). The appropriation of Latin American dances into North American social dance is a characteristic example of the latter taking over a dance from a culture it considers primitive (e.g., European peasantry, American blacks) in terms of that culture's more 'authentic' erotic expressivity. Identifying Hayworth with the style in the solo numbers in *Gilda* makes it possible to read her dancing in terms of eroticism for herself as well as for the spectator.

This reading is also made possible by the more general fact of Hayworth/Gilda's sexuality being importantly constructed in terms of movement. In her essay, 'Visual Pleasure and Narrative Cinema',[5] Laura Mulvey suggests an opposition between stasis and movement in relation to sexual objectification. The former fixes or controls the object of desire for the pleasurable gaze of the spectator, whereas the latter 'escapes' this control. Mulvey discusses this in terms of spectacle and narrative respectively, but one can also speak within the purely spectacular of sexual construction through stasis and movement. Significantly, by far the greater part of the history of women as sex objects in the cinema has been in terms of stasis – through the back-up industry of the pin-up (in this context, a most revealing term), through the isolation of specific fragments of the female body (Grable's legs, Lake's hair, Mansfield's breasts, etc.), through glamour photography that depends for its moulding and modulating effects on the stillness of the subject (cf., especially close-ups of the 'loved' one), and through 'choreographic' traditions that minimise movement (e.g., Busby Berkeley's patterned chorines, the slow haughty parade adopted from Ziegfeld, the use of the fashion show). In all these ways, the woman as sex object is fixed, held in place, controlled. Hayworth on the other hand is first seen cut in on a movement (tossing her hair back), a particularly dynamic effect, and her dance numbers are important moments in which the film dwells on her sexuality. In terms of the narrative, they are also moments of escape (borrowing generically from the musical), the first away from Johnny in Buenos Aires, the second defiantly and finally against him in his night club.

The fact of movement, the particular kind of movement, the association with it of Hayworth's image, its narrative placing, all make it possible to read Hayworth-as-Gilda either in Marjorie Rosen's terms:

> for the first time a heroine seemed to say, 'This is my body. It's lovely and gives me pleasure. I rejoice in it just as you do'.[6]

or else in terms of male heterosexual enjoyment of the character – of surrender rather than control. (There is after all no reason why heterosexual men should not enjoy in the cinema a sexual position – of passivity – that they are not supposed to enjoy, or be capable of, in actual heterosexual relations.)

Once we have pushed this far, however, we are close to suggesting that the film is far from placing Gilda/Hayworth as the unknowable against which to set Johnny/Ford as the known, and therefore as the validated masculine norm. On the contrary, according to this reasoning, it is Gilda/Hayworth who is known and normal, and Johnny who is unknown and deviant.

It is doubtful that most of us would come away with quite that conclusion. Generic conventions are very powerful as are more over-arching conventions, such as the happy heterosexual ending, in certain senses signalling Gilda/Hayworth's capitulation, and the fact that after all, Johnny/Ford is a man, already signifying masculinity and normality, just as Gilda/Hayworth as a woman already signifies femininity and deviance. As emerges from the discussions of the topic by Elizabeth Cowie and Griselda Pollock,[7] representations of women and men already powerfully signify the social place of women and men even before a film does anything with them.

Yet signification is never that fixed, and the narrative and star image procedures of *Gilda* do do some mischief with these normative conventions. There is a danger when making such a case of wanting to claim that we can therefore 'rescue' *Gilda* as a 'progressive' film. Perhaps we can, but it is worth noting at what price *Gilda* effects, in so far as it does, this construction of the female as normal over against the film noir hero. It is by suggesting that Johnny/Ford is not a 'real man', that he is in the position of the woman *vis-à-vis* Ballen, the camera and Gilda and that he is in some sense homosexual, that the construction of Hayworth-as-Gilda gains real force. The implication that Johnny is inadequate (also suggested by the overtones of sado-masochism in his relations with Ballen and Gilda) involves a criterion of adequacy. This can in part mean being like Gilda, but in this society it will still be notions of what real men are and should be like, that allow the film to place Johnny as inadequate. In other words, the film does in some measure expose its own problematic, whilst still holding on, at one further remove, to traditional notions of masculinity and normality.

Notes

1. Molly Haskell, *From Reverence to Rape,* Holt, Rinehart & Winston, New York 1974, p8, and Penguin, Baltimore 1974. For a critique of this position, see Claire Johnston, 'Feminist Politics and Film History', *Screen*, v16 n3, pp115-124.
2. Umberto Eco, 'Towards a Semiotic Enquiry into the Television Message', *Working Papers in Cultural Studies,* no. 3, Autumn 1972, p121.
3. 'According to Ford, the homosexual angle was obvious to them at the time: they could see the implications in the relationship between the men in the early part of the film – nothing stated, just mood . . .', John Kobal, 'The Time, the Place and the Girl: Rita Hayworth', *Focus on Film,* no. 10, p17.
4. I have discussed this aspect of the film in an article. 'Homosexuality and Film Noir', *Jump Cut,* no. 16, pp18-21.
5. Laura Mulvey, 'Visual Pleasure and Narrative Cinema', *Screen*, v16 n3, pp6-18.
6. Marjorie Rosen, *Popcorn Venus.* Avon Books, New York 1974, p226.
7 Elizabeth Cowie, 'Women, Representation and the Image', *Screen Education* no. 23, pp15-23; Griselda Pollock, 'What's Wrong with Images of Women?', *Screen Education*, no. 24, pp25-33.

Double Indemnity

Claire Johnston

Double Indemnity, based on James M. Cain's *roman noir* of the same title, is the story of an insurance agent, Walter Neff, who plots with Phyllis Dietrichson to kill her husband by making it appear that he died falling from a moving train, thus allowing them to claim double the insurance money on his life. In attempting to retain James M. Cain's first person interior monologue Billy Wilder and Raymond Chandler, the scriptwriter, used the narrative device, extremely rare in classic Hollywood cinema in the 1940s, of having Neff recite the past events into a dictaphone, so that the plot resolution is known from the outset, the film taking the form of a memory. Such a device at one level would seem to constitute an attempt to preserve the essence of the *roman noir* as a sub-genre of the detective genre as a whole.

As Todorov notes,[1] while retaining the structure of the enigma, the narrator displaces its centrality and relativises its structuring function within the narrative. In that the narrator does not know whether he will remain alive at the end, he becomes problematic for the reader. The *roman noir* fuses two narrative codes, suppressing the code of the detective story which offers the possibility of sense and believability for the reader in terms of an enigma resolved by the Law, and giving life to the first person narration spoken in the present coinciding with the action in the form of a memory. Essentially the *roman noir* as a sub-genre presents a particular social milieu of immorality and sordid crime in which the narrator risks his life and sanity.

The believability of the detective genre as a whole is a particular one founded on questions relating to the social construction of social reality – it is the character who is not suspected who is, in fact, guilty. Such a systematic process of inversion of social reality within the genre necessitates that social reality be re-affirmed through resolution and closure for the reader in terms of the Law. Far from opening up social contradictions, the genre as a whole, through such a process of naturalisation, performs a profoundly confirmatory function for the reader, both revealing and simultaneously eliminating the problematic aspects of social reality by the assertion of the unproblematic nature of the Law.

The use of the 'novelesque' in *Double Indemnity* as a continuous, first person narrative discourse co-extensive with the image track – semi-diegetic speech[2] – undoubtedly draws the film closer to literary speech, but within the filmic discourse its function within the text is displaced and transformed. While the film poses a first person narrating discourse which takes the form of a memory, the filmic/diegetic image is always in the present. Far from displacing the enigma in revealing the plot resolution at the beginning of the film, the first person narrative discourse, in its play of convergence/divergence with the visible, produces an enigma at another level for the viewer: a split relationship to knowledge. The first person narration presents itself as a 'confession' which reveals the truth of the narrative of events by which we can talk of the various characters in the film – it purports to provide the knowledge of how things really happened. But as the film unfolds, a divergence emerges between the knowledge which the first person narrative discourse provides and that which unfolds at the level of the visible. Finally, it is the visual discourse which serves as the guarantee of truth for the reader: 'the spectator can do no other than identify with the camera'.[3] In filmic discourse the relationship between the viewer and reality – the film – is one of pure specularity, in which the look of the spectator is denied, locking the spectator into a particular sense of identity.[4] Ultimately, classic Hollywood cinema is always in the third person – it is always objective – unless subjectivity is marked in the image itself (e.g., the blurred image of Gutman in *The Maltese Falcon*).[5] The narrative of events at the level of the visible provides the knowledge of how things really are and constitutes the dominant narrating instance.

In *Double Indemnity* the process of articulation between the narrating discourses at play is foregrounded by the 'novelesque' aspect of the genre itself, providing a complex interplay of convergence/divergence – a conflict at the level of the knowledges which the film provides for the viewer, setting in motion its own enigma. As the film progresses the narrator loses control of the narrative to the point where he himself comes under scrutiny. Keyes, the company claims investigator, the 'you' of Neff's first person narration, begins to investigate the case and Neff becomes a witness, subject to Keyes' investigation. It is the articulation of the 'I' and the 'you' of the first person narration (the relationship between the two men) with the narrative of events in the realm of the visible (the objective, third person process of narrativisation) which situates a split relationship to knowledge for the viewer and, with it, the enigma. At the centre of the enigma is the Oedipal trajectory of the hero – the problem of the knowledge of sexual difference in a patriarchal order.

The title sequence sets the film under the mark of castration: the silhouette of a male figure in hat and overcoat looms towards the camera on crutches. In the next sequence we see Walter Neff, injured and bleeding, entering the offices of his insurance company and begin his 'confession' to Keyes on the dictaphone. 'I killed Dietrichson – me, Walter Neff – insurance salesman – thirty five years old, no visible scars – till a while ago, that is . . . I killed him for money – and for a woman . . . It all began last May.'

It is to Keyes that Walter Neff's discourse, the 'I' of the voice-over, is addressed; a 'you' which is split between the Symbolic and the Imaginary[6] — a split that insists in the attempted overlapping of the functions of symbolic father and idealised father. Neff's opening 'confession' establishes Keyes as the representative of the Law — the symbolic father: 'you were right, but you got the wrong man'. As symbolic father, Keyes' unshakeable access to the truth, to knowledge, resides in his phallic attribute, his 'little man' which, by a process necessitated by censoring mechanisms, 'ties knots in his stomach', enabling him to spot a phoney claim instantly. His knowledge of the laws of mathematical probability, epitomised in his very name, enables him to chart the social excesses of the world and ensure the stability of property relations in the name of the insurance business. In the first scene in the claims office we see him interrogate a man with a phoney claim and render him an 'honest man' again. He describes his function within the institution as 'doctor', 'bloodhound', 'cop' and 'father confessor'.

As signifier of the patriarchal order, Keyes represents for Neff what it means to be capable of saying 'I am who I am', to be the one who knows; he is transcendent. In order to resolve the positive Oedipus and gain access to the Symbolic, the boy has to accept the threat of castration from the father. As Lacan has indicated, 'Law and repressed desire are one and the same thing'.[7] The Oedipus Complex allows access to desire only through repression: it is through lack that desire is instituted. As Keyes says of Neff: 'you're not smarter, you're just taller'. Neff's belief in Keyes' knowledge is absolute: 'you were right'. At the same time the Law always offers itself for transgression: the desire to 'con the system', to devise a scheme so 'perfect' that it can challenge the father's phallic function, his knowledge, and thus reduplicate the perfection of the system once more. But the symbolic father can only be imperfectly incarnate in the real father. As Neff's symbolic father, Keyes is marked by a lack, a blind spot. In the voice-over in the first scene in the claims office, Neff says (in retrospect) that he 'knew he had a heart as big as a house' — the reason why he 'got the wrong man'. It is the repressed, maternal side of Keyes which constitutes a blind spot for the patriarchal order, and it is this blind spot which for Neff sets in motion the desire for transgression which the son may always attempt against the father: to take his place.

Keyes also represents the idealised father for Neff: the ideal ego founded on narcissistic identifications constitutive of the realm of the Imaginary. As Freud indicated,[8] identifications in the pre-Oedipal phase are associated primarily with one's sexual like. The repressed homosexual desire of Neff for the idealised father rests on narcissistic identification, to 'think with your brains, Keyes', to possess his knowledge. In the all-male universe of the insurance business, women are seen as untrustworthy: as Keyes comments, they 'should be investigated' before any relationship is embarked on. Women represent the possibility of social excess which the insurance business seeks to contain — they 'drink from the bottle' (Keyes). The repressed, homosexual desire between the two men, the negative Oedipus, is symbolised by the visual rhyme, running throughout the film, of Neff's ritual lighting of Keyes' cigar as

102

Keyes fumbles each time for a match. This signifier is underpinned in the first scene in the claims office by Neff's words 'I love you, too' as Keyes jokingly threatens to throw his desk at him. Neff's pre-Oedipal, narcissistic identification with Keyes implies a disavowal rather than an acceptance of castration. Thus the film traces the precariousness of the patriarchal order and its internal contradictions precisely in this split between Symbolic and Imaginary symbolised in the place and function of Keyes in the fiction, and the inscription of castration for men within that order. Neff must both assume castration in a process of testing the Law so that he can take the place of the symbolic father, while, at the same time, disavowing castration in his narcissistic identifications with a father-figure – the idealised father.

As an example of the film noir, *Double Indemnity* poses a social reality constructed in the split, the interface, between the Symbolic and the Imaginary of a particular social order – that of the male universe of the insurance business – an order which activates/reactivates the trouble of castration for the male in patriarchy. It is in relation to the women in the film, to Phyllis Dietrichson/Barbara Stanwyck and her step-daughter Lola, that the internal contradictions of the patriarchal order (the Oedipal trajectory of male desire focused in Neff) are to be played out. The 'woman' is thus produced as the signifier of the lack, of heterogeneity – the 'fault' inherent in patriarchy as an order.

As Laura Mulvey has elaborated,[9] it is the contemplation of the female form which evokes castration anxiety for the male: the original trauma being the discovery that the mother is, in fact, not phallic, but castrated. As locus of lack/castration, as the site where radical difference is marked negatively, 'woman' is the pivot around which the circulation of male desire is played out in the text, and it is this process of circulation of desire which fixes the representation of women in the text. Phyllis Dietrichson/Barbara Stanwyck, celebrated female star and *femme fatale*, represents Neff's attempt to disavow castration in his repressed homosexuality and to test the Law, while Lola functions as the term in relation to which an acceptance of castration and the Symbolic Order is inscribed. As the narrative progresses, Phyllis Dietrichson/ Barbara Stanwyck gives way to Lola and the contradictions of the patriarchal order opened up by the film are contained for the next generation. It is Neff's paternal function in relation to Lola which restores her as good object within familial relations. The enigma of the problem of the knowledge of sexual difference is thus resolved by the Law *for* patriarchy.

In the scene immediately following Neff's 'confession' to Keyes, both Phyllis Dietrichson/Barbara Stanwyck and Lola are introduced into the narrative, as Neff goes to renew an insurance policy at the house. His voice-over fixes them as memory, *as already known*, in the 'I' and 'you' discourse between the two men. In a dusty semi-darkened room Phyllis Dietrichson/Barbara Stanwyck, covered in a bath towel, stands at the top of the stairs offered to and held in the mastery of Neff's gaze. Neff jokes that she might not be 'fully covered' by the insurance policy on the car: the hint of social excess. At the same time

the voice-over draws our attention to the photograph on the piano of
Dietrichson and his daughter by his first marriage, Lola. Visually, the women
resemble each other in age and general appearance in a striking way. 'Mother'
and 'daughter' are nevertheless, from the beginning, established as inhabiting
a different space in the diegesis, Phyllis Dietrichson/Barbara Stanwyck frozen
as fetish object in Neff's look, already outside the space of familial relations,
and Lola frozen in the family photograph from which Phyllis is excluded.

The initial shots of Neff's encounter with Phyllis Dietrichson/Barbara
Stanwyck are marked by a fetishistic fascination: simultaneously the dangerous site of castration and the pleasurable appearance – the object of the look
– she is the source of reassuring pleasure in the face of castration anxiety.
The 'I' of the voice-over talks of this fascination, converging with the 'I' of the
look: the viewer is thus drawn into a fetishistic split between belief and knowledge. As she begins to come down the stairs of the California-style Spanish
house, we see a close-up of her legs and her golden anklet. The camera follows
Neff and catches his image in the mirror as he watches her finish buttoning up
her dress and putting on her lipstick. She turns from the mirror, leaving him
still fixed in his gaze, and moves over to the other side of the room.

His privileged look at her exhibitionism in the mirror shot, a moment of
pure specularity, marks a disjuncture between his look and that of the viewer:
imprisoned in his narcissistic identifications, the identity of Neff and viewer is
simultaneously doubled, split and recomposed – his gaze becomes uneasy. He
must investigate the woman further and discover her guilty secret in his desire
to test the Law. The possibility of social excess which she represents, her

incongruity as suburban housewife, suggests her as a vehicle for his Oedipal transgression. She asks him about accident insurance for her husband and he flirts with her, continuing the driving metaphor around the car insurance, to discover more. She says he's 'going too fast'. He leaves, making an appointment to call the next day.

The following scene of his visit to the house the next day is dominated by shots of Neff watching her as he tries to discover her guilty secret. We see her descend the stairs to open the door as the voice-over recalls her anklet: the mastery of his gaze is re-presented as a memory image. He asks her to call him Walter and offers to run the vacuum cleaner. As he watches, she tells him about the boredom of her married life and asks him about taking out accident insurance on her husband's life. He interrogates her and asks her why she married her husband. The camera remains on his face as she asks how she could take out the accident insurance without either her husband or the company knowing. He tells her how it could be done and says, as he leaves, she 'can't get away with it'. In the voice-over Neff says, 'I knew I had hold of a red hot poker and it was time to drop it before it burned my hand off'. The images confirm his complicity for the viewer, his sadistic play with the woman.

As Laura Mulvey notes,[10] the disavowal of castration for the male in its fascination and the desire to know her guilty secret is fundamentally sadistic — it must also involve her punishment. Phyllis Dietrichson/Barbara Stanwyck, entombed in the domesticity of the Spanish house, represents the possibility of a libidinal satisfaction which cannot be contained within the Symbolic Order and the structure of familial relations. For the patriarchal order founded on castration, she is a trouble which can be spoken about but not acted upon. As such, she encapsulates the concerns of the film noir itself — that (as Neff says in the voice-over) 'murder can sometimes smell like honeysuckle'. In her very impossibility, she offers herself as a vehicle for Neff to test the Law, but the erotic drives she represents must finally, in the film noir, become subject to the Law — she must be found guilty and punished. These drives can only be destructive and lead to death, in that she represents, precisely, the heterogeneity which must form the outside of the Symbolic Order, the excluded that allows the order to exist as an order.[11]

The love scene necessitates the confession of her guilty secret — that which troubles the order and which will have to be worked through in and by the text: 'it was only the beginning . . .' (Neff). The bell rings and she stands in a pool of light, offered to the gaze of Neff and viewer, in the doorway of Neff's darkened apartment. The voice-over suggests an appointment which the image denies: 'it would be eight and she would be there'. She is holding his hat and is returning it. Later they embrace on the sofa and he draws her into confessing her guilty secret — that she would like her husband dead. As they embrace, their love-making is elided by the camera tracking out of the apartment room and, in the next shot, into Neff's office as he tells Keyes on the dictaphone that he always wanted to 'con the system'. The camera then tracks back out of the office and back into the apartment room to find them

again on the sofa. Sexual knowledge of the woman and Neff's Oedipal trajectory, *vis-à-vis* Keyes, to test the Law, are held and relocated diegetically for
the viewer in this relocation of sex with Phyllis into the verbal interchange
with Keyes. As she begins to leave, Neff agrees to help her to get her husband
to sign the insurance papers. As we hear the car drive away, Neff's voice-over
says 'the machinery had started to move'; he would have to 'think with your
brains, Keyes', assume mastery of the Symbolic Order, the system, in order to
explore its interstices.

At this point the sexual drives opened up by the woman and the need for
narcissistic identification with the father come into contradiction. We return
to Neff's office and the 'confession' to Keyes on the dictaphone, as Neff tells
him he 'didn't like the witness' to Dietrichson's signature, how he felt 'queer
in the belly'. There is a fade to Lola's image sitting in mid-shot playing
Chinese chequers. The transition emphasises Lola's position on the side of
mastery within the order which Neff is testing for gaps – in this sense, Lola is
on the side of Keyes. As witness she represents the social order encapsulated
in the persona of Keyes: the containment of social excess and the regulation
of property relations. The camera tracks out from Lola to reveal the family
scene, and as Dietrichson signs the documents, her image remains central in
the frame. Neff's eyes follow her as she goes upstairs.

The threat to Neff which Lola represents is precisely her centrality within
the family, her role of daughter, subject to the Law of the Father. As witness,
she functions as a reference to, a sign of, the Symbolic Order which he seeks

106

to transgress — she's a 'nice kid'. He leaves the house, and arrives at his car to find her sitting in the front seat. At this point there is a disturbance in the point-of-view structure in the text. She asks him to give her a lift into town, and confides in him that she is secretly going to see her boyfriend, Nino. Neff's attitude is paternal. As he drops her off in town the voice-over comments: 'the father was a dead pigeon'.

In order to simulate Dietrichson's death from a moving train and claim the double indemnity on his life, Neff has to take his place. In so doing he not only becomes Phyllis's 'husband', but Lola's 'father'. In destroying the family unit, in testing the Law, Neff has entered an impossible family, a family explicitly based on a sacrificial murder, and thus socially censored. After murdering Dietrichson and taking his place on the train his desire vanishes: having successfully achieved a replica of the family, he is now in the position of the master in an *other* symbolic order, one that exists alongside and in the face of the social order represented by Keyes. The car fails to start: he and Phyllis part on a reluctant embrace. On the way to the drug store, after establishing his alibi, Neff's voice-over says: 'I couldn't hear my own foot-steps . . . it was the walk of a dead man'. The impossible family is a nightmare. Neff exists in a no-man's-land.

In committing the 'perfect' crime, he and Phyllis now exist outside the certitude of the Symbolic Order represented in the legality of the insurance contract signed by Dietrichson. They can no longer meet at the house, and have to meet at the supermarket. The libidinal drives which Phyllis represents can only lead to her death: she is guilty and will be punished. Keyes' 'little man' will tell him something is wrong. But Neff can rely on Keyes' blind spot, his maternal side, the 'fault' in the Symbolic Order. Neff knows he has a 'heart as big as a house'. Outside the symbolic, Neff remains, nevertheless, subject to the Law: Keyes' relentless scrutiny of the insurance claim and the look of the camera, this time on Neff, as the investigation proceeds.

At this point in the film, the balance in which Phyllis and Lola are held in relation to Neff begins to change in terms of spatial relationships at the level of the visible. Keyes comes to Neff's apartment to tell him that he suspects Phyllis and that he intends to 'put her through the wringer'. Phyllis has come to see Neff and is hiding behind the door as Keyes leaves to get something to ease his stomach. Before he gets to the elevator, he takes out a cigar and turns to Neff for his ritual light. The shot encapsulates a change in the direction of Neff's Oedipal trajectory, with Phyllis foregrounded behind the door in darkness and the men in the light of the hallway on the other side of the door. When Keyes leaves, Phyllis complains that Neff is 'going off her'. They embrace and there is a fade and transition (for the first time without the voice-over to signal it) which completes this change in direction, revealing Lola waiting outside Neff's office: 'do you remember me, Mr. Neff? . . . look at me, Mr. Neff'. The camera underpins his look at the witness.

Lola says she knows Phyllis is guilty and is going 'to tell': she threatens to interrupt Neff's confessional voice-over to Keyes. She will become the narra-tor and break the imaginary duality of the Neff/Keyes relationship. She says she has moved out of the house and is living alone: the scene ends on a close-up of her tearful face. As 'father', Neff must return the 'daughter' to the safety of familial relations. As the voice-over tells us how he had decided to take her out to 'keep her quiet', we see a series of two-shots, idyllic images of happiness, as they eat in candlelight at a restaurant and go driving in the countryside. At the discursive level, the voice-over no longer provides the truth with which to read the image. In the transition from Phyllis to Lola, unmarked by Neff's voice-over and visible in terms of spatial relationships, Phyllis gives way to Lola and the Symbolic Order which she represents returns, threatening from within the replica of the family which has been constructed.

From now on the metaphor of the car is replaced by that of the 'trolley ride'. Having established Phyllis' guilt, Keyes is now looking for her accomplice – the 'other person'. As Keyes says: 'they are on a trolley ride together and the last stop is the cemetery'. Desire which cannot be contained within the Symbolic Order (the trouble represented by Phyllis) can only lead to death, in that it represents the outside of that order, that which must be repressed or contained if that order is to continue to exist. As Keyes says, 'They are digging their own graves'. In the supermarket scene, Phyllis continues Keyes' metaphor: 'It's straight down the line for both of us, remember?'

The inexorable link between desire and death is relocated diegetically for the viewer as we return to Neff's office and the dictaphone: 'It was the first time I thought of Phyllis that way – dead, I mean, and how it would be if she were dead'. Continuing, he says how at that moment he thought of Lola, and there is a transition to a series of shots of their trip to the Hollywood Bowl. As they sit in two-shot, Lola's back is to the camera and, in the darkness, the physical resemblance to Phyllis is striking. Phyllis, already as good as dead, is replaced by Lola, restoring 'woman' as good object for the patriarchal order: the trouble is contained in its rightful place.

Having acknowledged the impossibility of his Oedipal trajectory, the narrator loses control of the narrative. The voice-over can no longer hold the narrative of events, and becomes questioning and uncertain. Keyes' investigation, inaugurating a counter-discourse to the narrative discourse of Neff's 'I', structured around the enigma of 'that sombody else', comes to hold the process of narrativisation for the viewer. This resituating of the 'I' and the 'you' of the narrative discourse is underpinned in the scene where Neff, thinking Keyes is double-crossing him, goes to Keyes' office and listens on the dictaphone to Keyes' confidential memo on his investigation of him, to discover that Keyes 'personally vouches for him'. The rhyme of the dictaphone asserts the 'you' at the level of the visible, at the same time confirming Keyes' blind spot: he doesn't see Neff's culpability. Having come to occupy the place of the father against the Symbolic Order, and discovered its impossibility, Neff must 'get rid of the whole mess' – Phyllis. 'Woman', locus of castration, of anxiety, the source of the 'whole mess', must be punished: he must 'get off the trolley car' before its logical end.

The rhyme of Phyllis's legs descending the stairs, now no longer caught in the mastery of his gaze, introduces the final flashback scene at the house. We see her descend, holding a gun wrapped in a chiffon scarf, unlock the door and put the gun under a cushion. She pursues her function in relation to the order whose excess she is and reaffirms her guilt still further. She says she is 'rotten to the heart' and that she is trying to persuade Lola's boyfriend, Nino, to 'take care of Lola'. Neff circles round her as she speaks. He walks to the window to shut it and she shoots him. He staggers towards her telling her to try again. The camera is held on her as she drops the gun and moves into a close-up as they embrace. She confesses that she never loved him but that she couldn't fire the second shot. As they remain locked in their embrace, he shoots her: she looks surprised. The eroticisation of death in the final scene of the flashback confirms a universe where access to desire is only through repression: the impossibility of a radical heterogeneity represented by the feminine.

Mortally wounded, Neff leaves the house; he meets Nino and gives him a nickel to ring Lola and make it up with her, restoring, symbolically, the *status quo ante*. The flashback ends and we return to Neff's office and the dictaphone. He ends his message to Keyes by asking him to take care of Lola and Nino. The 'father' restores the 'daughter' to the Symbolic Order and familial relations. 'Woman' as good object is reinstated for the next generation. The patriarchal order is now reaffirmed, and with it the internal contradictions for the male universe of the insurance business. The trouble of castration for the male in patriarchy as it insists in the disjunction between the Symbolic and the Imaginary fathers is reactivated. As Neff finishes his message to Keyes, the camera angle suggests a subjective look. It is the look of the 'you' to whom the 'I' has been addressed. Neff turns and acknowledges Keyes' presence. When asked why he couldn't 'figure it out', Keyes acknowledges his blind spot: 'You can't figure them all, Walter'. Neff asks for four hours' grace to cross 'the border'. Keyes replies that he won't even reach the elevator: he's 'all washed up'.

The split between the Symbolic and the Imaginary which structures the text insists in Keyes' overlapping function as symbolic and idealised father, driving the film towards resolution and closure. As symbolic father Keyes must represent the Law and hand Neff over to the police. As idealised father there remains the problem of narcissistic identification, and with it, repressed homosexuality – 'the border'.

The camera holds the two men in frame and follows Neff as he staggers towards the glass doors of his office while Keyes, now out of frame, speaks on the telephone: 'It's a police job'. Keyes then walks into frame as Neff lies slumped against the door and kneels beside him. Neff says: 'I know why you couldn't figure this one . . . because the guy you were looking for was too close . . . right across the desk from you'. Keyes replies: 'Closer than that, Walter', to which Neff gives his customary ironic reply: 'I love you, too'. As Neff lies dying he gets out a cigarette and the rhyme completes the mutual confession: Keyes returns Neff's ritual gesture and lights the cigarette. Having handed over his function as symbolic father to the police, Keyes can now acknowledge and return Neff's love in the signifier of repressed desire. The challenge to the patriarchal order eliminated and the internal contradictions of that order contained, a sublimated homosexuality between the men can now be signified. But there can be no more words – only The End.

Notes

1. *The Poetics of Prose*, Blackwell, Oxford 1977, pp42-52.
2. Christian Metz, 'Current Problems of Film Theory', *Screen*, v14 ns 1/2, Spring/ Summer 1973, p69.
3. Christian Metz, 'History/Discourse: Note on two voyeurisms', *Edinburgh '76 Magazine*, p23.
5. Stephen Heath, 'Narrative Space', *Screen*, v17 n2, Autumn 1976, p93.
6. For an account of the psychoanalytic framework to which these terms belong, see Rosalind Coward, 'Lacan and signification: an introduction', *Edinburgh '76 Magazine*.
7. Jacques Lacan, *Ecrits*, Editions du Seuil, Paris 1966, p782; a selection from *Ecrits* has been translated by Tavistock Press, London 1977.
8. 'Instincts and their Vicissitudes', *Collected Papers*, Hogarth Press, London 1951, p65.
9. 'Visual Pleasure and Narrative Cinema', *Screen*, v16 n3, Autumn 1975, p13.
10. Ibid., p14.
11. See Julia Kristeva, 'Signifying Practice and Mode of Production', *Edinburgh '76 Magazine*.
12. Ibid.

Klute 2: feminism and *Klute*

Christine Gledhill

What is at stake for feminist analysis in examining *Klute* in terms of film noir? For instance a persuasive account of the film is given by Diane Giddis in which she not only makes Bree the central figure of the film, but converts the two male characters into symbolic extensions of the heroine's divided self:

> The film functions on both levels, as a straight suspense story and as a dramatisation of intense inner conflict, but it is from the second level that it derives its power.[1]

In other words she is prepared to ignore the conventions of film noir, as *mere* conventions which simply carry a deeper revelation of one of the 'greatest contemporary female concerns: the conflict between the claims of love and the claims of autonomy' (p57). But from the discussions of the location of women within film noir in this pamphlet, I hope it is clear that conventions have at least a structuring role, placing constraints on the production of the female image. An analysis which observes these conventions reappropriated in the name of contemporary exploration, and assimilated to the stylistic needs of modern cinema, enables us to bring into sharper focus the strategies and conventions of that cinema, often less discernible for their modernity, and so perhaps to become a little clearer about the operation of patriarchal ideology in current film-making.

This is all the more vital a need in the case of *Klute* which puts Jane Fonda – the star famous for her change of image from sex object to 'serious' politicised roles under pressure from her growing political consciousness – in the role occupied by the *femme fatale* or evil woman in the forties film noir. This role is now defined in more upfront sexual terms as the prostitute – although a prostitute with ambitions to become an actress. In other words the film is trying to articulate, within the ambience of the thriller, a modern version of the independent woman, conceived of as the sexually liberated, unattached, hip woman and so without mentioning feminism or women's

112

liberation arguably trying to cash in on these concerns to enhance the modernity of the type. At the same time the film locates the heroine's dilemma within a contemporary moral and sexual malaise, articulated in the archetypal opposition of country/city but dressed in updated terms – attacking the libertarian, hippie counter-culture of the sixties as decadent, morally corrupt, and psychically alienated.

In fact, as I hope to show, the ideological project surrounding this version of the independent woman stereotype is the same as when it emerged in the 1890s under the guise of the 'New Woman', namely to show that however fascinating, different, admirable the would-be emancipated woman, struggling to assert her own identity in a male world, and professing a new, non-repressive and sexual morality, in the end she is really neurotic, fragile, lonely and unhappy. I would argue that *Klute*'s production of the stereotype is no different in its ultimate effect, and that the film operates in a profoundly anti-feminist way, perhaps even more so than the forties thrillers from which it derives.

To begin to substantiate this proposition we need to examine how it is that in Diane Giddis's words the 'greatest contemporary female concerns' are articulated within the thriller and what happens to them in the process. I would argue that Pakula's ambition to explore contemporary issues within the framework of the genre, together with his modernisation of the genre, works on those conventions to wrest them out of their formulaic nature and turn them into conscious metaphors for the 'human condition' assimilable to contemporary concerns.

For this reason it is perfectly feasible for Diane Giddis to discover within the functioning of the thriller a story about female problems which evokes a powerful sense of recognition, and part of my ultimate disagreement with her analysis of the film is an ideological one with her estimation of what she recognises.

However, such an evaluation is made more likely by the critical tradition she draws on, which, by demanding that the critic reconstitute the film's meaning as a coherent expression of a world view, allows her to read all the film's operations in terms of the heroine's subjectivity as the unifying principle. The terms of this unification are then provided by the metaphors of the human condition with which the European cinematic tradition abounds.

The point is that to constitute all the items of filmic production as metaphors for a meaning in an over-arching discourse – the exploration of the human condition etc. – leads away from their particular ideological effects within the organisation of the text to a system of values constituted outside the film, which may not actually speak for the critic's ostensible interest.

This is not to suggest that a 'correct reading' is to be discovered only 'inside' the film. Any reading, whether thematic or what I'd loosely call 'structural', is bound to be carried out from a particular reading position, and both Diane Giddis and I work from within a feminist perspective. But the issue is how such a perspective is to be articulated in terms of critical practice.

Diane Giddis's feminism leads her straight to the heroine's subjectivity, which, without considering the twists and turns of plot, character, formal device etc., she takes the rest of the film as expressing. This then puts on her the onus of reconstructing the psychology of 'The Divided Woman' which in turn diverts her from the feminist proposition that the problems for women of entering personal relationships are as much to do with the forms those relations have to take in a patriarchal, capitalist society, as with the seemingly eternal psychological differences between the sexes — the tenet of the tradition she is using. This then leads her to a conclusion, the implications of which are at odds with feminism, namely, that women must put more of their identity and independence at risk in personal, heterosexual relationships than men.

On the other hand to focus on textual operations means both bearing in mind the kind of reading the film invites us to make according to traditional critical values and refusing their elaboration; instead the critic looks at the structural relations between different aspects of the text which cannot be turned directly into a 'meaning' but which affect or produce implications for the placing of woman in the film — 'woman' being understood here not as an individualised character, but as a cultural and social category which in its turn has a structuring effect on the place actual concrete women find themselves in within patriarchal society. A key notion for this argument is point of view. Diane Giddis asserts:

> *Klute* is told from a highly subjective viewpoint and the other characters, while 'real', can be seen as projections of the heroine's psyche. (p57)

The critical methodology by which Diane Giddis goes straight to the film's immanent meaning means she does not have to ask how point of view is constructed in the cinema or within specific genres. But in my discussion of point of view in film noir I have suggested that the structural location of women within the film text may have very different implications from the meanings derived by interpreting the film in terms of a character. Point of view is an effect structured into the text by a number of different operations and is not simply the result of thematic emphasis. Perhaps this seems a little unfair to Diane Giddis's argument, for she does follow this observation with a convincing account of the parallelism between Klute and Cable of which she says:

> In fact, that threat, Bree's potential killer, can be seen as the incarnation of the emotional danger presented by Klute. From the beginning the two men are almost always shown in juxtaposition. The morning after Bree receives a 'breather' call from her tormentor, Klute makes his first appearance in her life. (p57)

But while within Diane Giddis's terms this reading makes thematic sense it is difficult to see how this relation between the two men is established in the filmic operation of the text as the expression of Bree's subjectivity. Rather, if we trace the play of noir conventions within this Europeanised production it seems more feasible to say Bree is the object in a struggle between two different male constructions on female sexuality and that the discourse of woman is severely restricted.

Again what is at stake for feminist film criticism in stating this disagreement? It is not merely a question of posing a 'correct' reading against a less complete one, for although analysis of textual operations produces implications for meaning, it is not concerned to come out with a coherent interpretation, a reconstitution of the text in terms of an overall meaning. As far as *Klute* is concerned *textual analysis* requires in the first place *not* following the film's invitation to separate the level of 'serious issues' from the level of the detective story, seen simply as metaphoric support of a world-view. Rather we are required to reconstitute sets of textual operations: *first*, the specific determinations on the female image carried out by the conventions and devices of the noir thriller and, *second*, the fictional and stylistic conventions emanating from the European art movie as genre, which make the presence of 'serious issues' available to recognition and the work they perform on the female image. It may then be possible to show how the articulation together of the two traditions – the noir thriller and the European art movie – produces a structure in which the problem posed by Women's Liberation is displaced onto the 'trouble' the female image constitutes for the former – the film noir – only to be recuperated and resolved in terms of the moral perspectives of the latter – the European tradition.

The result of this process is that the disturbances, inconsistencies and dislocations of the noir thriller are diminished, if not harmonised and the place of the woman is relocated in far less threatening terms, her image reduced · and brought under control at far less cost to the male psyche than happens in the noir thriller.

An analysis of the place of woman in *Klute*

As we have noted *Klute* recasts some of the traditions of the noir thriller and seeks to assimilate them within an exploration of the contemporary condition. Pakula aims both for stylisation, the dramatic potential of the genre, and the revelation of a certain truth (see above, p20). In this respect he has more self-conscious, more seriously 'artistic' ambitions than did the genre workers who produced the noir thrillers of the forties and fifties. He doesn't want simply to reproduce the genre but to rework it to his own ends. What does Pakula take from film noir? How does he assimilate what he takes to contemporary conventions? What consequences do these choices have for the location of woman?

Narrative structure

To begin with those features of film noir which I have suggested are crucial to its ambiguous location of women, its particular investigative narrative structure and consequent thematic organisation.

First, the *investigative structure:* the *family* and the *heroine* form a set of relations that resemble aspects of the noir plot and at the same time exhibit striking differences. These relations are initiated in the pre-credit opening sequence of the film. The investigation starts out from an Edenic and pastoral image of the family: husband and wife in intimate rapport amongst a gathering of friends joining together in an open-air meal. A leap in time, an empty chair, the father is missing, and illicit sex appears to have broken the family up. The only evidence of Tom Gruneman's whereabouts is a foul letter he has written a prostitute, whom he is supposed to have beaten up.

The wife's loyal denials of the suggestion that her husband is 'a very sick man' are juxtaposed to the mystery shot of a tape recorder which opened the film — now playing back the voice of Bree Daniels, the film's prostitute heroine, calmly recommending her client unashamedly to act out his desires: 'Don't be ashamed, nothing is wrong, let it all hang out.' Thus the image of the family is dislodged by the voice of a woman activating sex, and will only be evoked for three more brief moments: by the pimp, Frank Ligourin's, parodic reference to his 'family' of whores; by John Klute's enquiry to Cable about the people back home; and by Bree's final ironic dismissal of domesticity. So John Klute, an old family friend and ex-policeman who has undertaken to search for Tom Gruneman, will have to travel from the Tuscororan countryside to New York and start his investigation by seeking out the prostitute who may or may not have led the missing man astray. From there he will go on to uncover the moral decadence and sexual alienation of city life.

Thus sexuality is central to the ex-policeman's investigation, and the dominant images of the criminal ambience and investigation in *Klute* — the tape recorder, the telephone, phone-calls from 'breathers', bugging — suggest a prying search into areas of private life and its personal secrets, rather than the plottings of criminal organisations. The psycho-sexual dimension of this privacy is further emphasised by the vertical camera-work,[2] sudden plummeting downward zooms, or ascensions in liftshafts, and by an imagery of netting, wire mesh, and claustrophobic rooms made vulnerable by skylights, and suggesting insecurity, sudden submersion, imprisonment.

But already crucial differences stand out indicating the way in which noir traditions are being re-articulated to mesh in with contemporary cinematic conventions and ideological emphases. A major change is the absence of the flashback structure and a consequent relocation of the past. Absence of the flashback produces a major change in the relation of the investigator/hero to his task of uncovering events. For a start he does not have to reflect on his own actions. Secondly the process of detection remains important in plot terms in that the criminal activity is still proceeding into the future and there is still a possibility of Gruneman's being discovered alive and well. Consequently there is a much more straightforward linear drive to the narration of events, more chance of the hero's gaining control over them, with none of the circularity, reversals and gaps of the typical forties noir plot.

116

How then does this more mainstream detective construction accommodate the investigation of sexuality which seems central to film noir? To begin with the place of the woman in the criminal complex is different. She is not the instrument of Tom Gruneman's fate but rather a clue on the way to its discovery. Thus the structural relation of the detective to the heroine is very different from what is usually the case in a classic film noir. Thus although the relation Klute establishes with the prostitute supersedes solution of the crime in importance — indeed, the identity of the murderer is given away very early in the film to facilitate this — it is not itself at the centre of the criminal problem. Rather the development of the relationship takes a parallel course to the process of detection, which, rather than being submerged in the sexual relations set up by the plot as in classic film noir, retains a distinct if skeletal outline. This disengagement of the criminal problem (albeit a sexual one) from the relationship between the detective and heroine means that this relationship is freed of the psychopathic quality it has in the forties thriller, so that Pakula, in the tradition of the European art movie, is able to use it as a means of exploring the serious contemporary issues he wants to accommodate within the thriller.

Of greater interest to us, however, is a shift in sexual emphases between the plot's various roles. In the forties thriller the great issue in question is the reliability or otherwise of the woman, the degree of fidelity or treachery inherent in her sexuality. In *Klute* the myth of woman as sexual instigator or predator is very quickly undermined, in the early scenes that document her life, scenes I will discuss in detail later. Here, however, John Klute's mission is in the first instance to establish his friend's honour, the sexual integrity of the man. And in the course of using the prostitute to help him gain access to the city's sexual haunts, he develops a protective attitude towards her too, and far from seeking to expose the evil of her sexuality, his desire is to save her. But before we go further into this re-inflected characterisation of the detective/hero, we need, as a necessary context, to look more closely at the investigative structure of *Klute*.

Patterns of investigation in *Klute*

There are at least four variations on the investigatory/confessional pattern in *Klute*, which can be schematised as follows:

1.

Klute and Cable are both spying on Bree Daniels, the prostitute. Cable, because it was his encounter with Bree and her permissive counter-culture philosophy — 'nothing is wrong, let it all hang out' — which first led him to locate all the evils of the world and male back-sliding with women. Armed with a tape recorder, he compiles a morbid dossier on the moral decadence

117

into which he sees Bree and her associates leading men, and is conducting a private campaign of terror against the women which culminates in the ultimate punishment, murder. Klute is spying on Bree first as a detective, because it is only through Bree's work as prostitute that he can hope to trace the client, known for beating up call girls, who is reputed to be Tom Gruneman; later, however, he keeps watch as a protector, wanting to save Bree from unknown intruders.

2.

A circular investigation, in which Cable employs Klute, a friend of the Gruneman family, to search for its head whom he himself has murdered; in other words he initiates an investigation into himself, an investigation which forces him to hasten the completion of his work, his final confrontation with Bree, in which he makes his confessional accusations against her, laying his three murders at her door, and claiming, that, as he is not an evil man, the blame must be hers.

3. B
   ⟩ psychotherapist
   B

This confessionally oriented investigation represents the noir investigation of female sexuality but divorced from the male hero and instigated by the woman herself. Bree recognises her sexual activity as a prostitute as a kind of sickness, wishes to find its origins and effect a cure. This structure dominates the interpretative field of the film. If there is any sense of dislocation between the different discourses of the film, it is between the on-going dialogue of prostitute and psychotherapist in juxtaposition with the detective-story. But the effect of such dislocation is to draw attention to the psychotherapeutic discourse as the key to the other investigatory structures, demanding they be read in psycho-spiritual terms. This does not mean, however, that the psychotherapist takes over from the detective in providing the answers as I shall try to show later; but that the metaphoric power of noir *conventions* is brought into more conscious play, enabling the film to do the work of a 'serious exploration of contemporary life' rather than generic entertainment. Above all it is a structure that re-articulates the *femme fatale* stereotype of film noir to bring it in line with contemporary female stereotypes and in so doing, I would argue, contributes to the neutralisation of the female threat to patriarchy.

4. The final investigative structure cannot be schematised so neatly as the preceding ones and does not concern characters, but rather represents the picaresque elements in a certain kind of detective story, developed more

recently in the police movie (*Dirty Harry, Magnum Force, Coogan's Bluff*, TV police serials) in which the lone investigating hero's pursuit of the criminal leads him into a descent into the underside of city life, reminiscent of Bunyan's Vanity Fair where each door that is opened displays a tableau representing one further aspect of the city's decadence and corruption – e.g., the hippies, pot-smoking in the basement of Bree's apartment building; the visit to the high-class madame, and then the downbeat Mama Reese's; the two desperate junkies, awaiting their connection; the disco-dive, where Bree puts herself once more under the protection of her ex-pimp Frank Ligourin; the pimp's flat where he poses as a high-class photographer, living off the earnings of his *ersatz* family etc. It is a city located not in a socio-economic system but in a moral sphere, and condemned for its abandonment to desperate hedonism, material acquisition, indulgent self-expression, perverted pleasures.

John Klute – detective-hero

If we look at the way these patterns of investigation relate to each other we can see a change in the organisation of the classic noir plot in that the hero's role of investigating and evaluating female sexuality is split, first between Klute and Cable and second between Klute and the psychotherapist. The effect of this, as I have already suggested, is to facilitate a separation of the plot motives of detection and passion. Because of where the heroine is placed in the criminal investigation, the detective is relieved of the burden of judgement on her, which now lies with the criminal himself, whose role, consequently, assumes much larger proportions in the plot. The articulation together of the two patterns of investigation associated with Klute and Cable means that at the point where the detective is becoming involved with the heroine, she is cleared of direct involvement in the crime (Klute hands Bree back her tapes) and in fact she comes to the hero's aid. Thus the fatal passion of film noir, relieved of criminality, can be humanised into a love-story, which is helped into being by the psychotherapist. At the same time the heroine's guilt is redefined as Cable's investigation bears more heavily on her life and the detective hero is able to take up the role of saviour. The roles of the psychotherapist and Cable I will deal with in more detail later. Here I want to look at how the narrative reorganisation of the role of the noir hero effects a re-articulation of his stereotype and characterisation, and the consequent placing of the heroine in relation to him.

Two features dominate this characterisation, both of which serve to distinguish Klute from his forerunners: silence, and a puritanical, almost virginal sexuality. Like the forties noir investigator, Klute is a loner, an outsider and a stern moralist; however, the origins of his moral rectitude are different. Rather than deriving from cynicism built on an embittered and disillusioned experience of the world, Klute's power stems from his innocence – a country boy, with his illusions and morals intact; his qualification for the task of searching for Gruneman is that 'he's interested, he cares'. Indeed the plot goes out of its way to disqualify him in police terms, for he has no experience of 'missing persons work'. Klute's innocent puritanism also distinguishes him sexually from his predecessors in the noir thriller. While the forties private eye moralised against the *femme fatale*, he was too cynical not to take what she offered and through this she could exercise some power. Klute, however, is markedly virginal, bluntly refusing Bree's offer of her body in exchange for the tapes he has made of her phonecalls and withholding sex on other occasions where the forties private-eye might be expected to take advantage of the availability of the heroine; for instance, the night an intruder appears above the skylight, he sits up all night in a chair by her bedside and later, when she goes to his basement flat afraid, he offers her his bed while he sleeps on a spare mattress.

Thus a further structural change takes place in the relation of hero and heroine in the noir thriller. Rather than the hero reluctantly succumbing to the heroine's first sexual initiatives, Klute's puritanism undermines her confident sexual assertiveness and she has to wait till he is asleep before seducing him. Bree and Klute first make love after she has gone frightened and waif-like during the night to his basement room to ask for his company and comfort. This is a scene very uncharacteristic of sexual encounter in film noir, all eroticism played down with Bree in an old mac and men's pyjamas, yet sandwiched between scenes of 'aberrant' sexuality that have incurred Klute's stern, disapproving gaze – first their visits to Bree's former mentor, the high-class madame who offers her a home any time she is in need, and to the disco where Bree meets some apparently lesbian friends in search of Jane McKenna; following this scene, their visit to Mama Reese's, where they find prostitutes draped over fat middle-aged businessmen. Thus the force of Klute's moral rectitude, which places these city-life tableaux, and others like them, as decadent, is characterised as something totally other, different from the values of the world he scrutinises, and not founded on disillusioned experience of this world as is the morality of the forties noir hero. This is reinforced by a further difference: whereas the hard-boiled investigators of the forties thrillers are remarkable for their cynical, wise-cracking repartee and commentary on events – something the voice-over technique indulges – Klute is characterised by an inscrutable silence. Such silence is facilitated by the picaresque, tableau-like structure to the detective strands of the plot, but marks even scenes of personal relationship where dialogue might be expected. More will be said about Klute's silence later.

In place of the brutalism of the forties hard-boiled hero, Klute's moral disgust at the sexual permissiveness and general decadence of the city is tempered by mothering qualities which respond not to Bree's sexuality but to the lost child in her. He protects her when she is frightened, puts her to bed when she is freaked out, tidies up her flat, chooses her the best fruit in the market. But Klute's gentleness in no way undermines his masculinity. In case this might be in doubt after his refusal of Bree's sexual advances in her flat, he is immediately given the opportunity to demonstrate his male authority, through his command of the situation when he hears somebody above the skylight of Bree's flat, and in the course of a rooftop to basement pursuit pulls his gun – something which he doesn't then have to do till the final confrontation with Cable at the end of the film. Klute's gentleness is accompanied by strong paternalistic traits. Twice his protectiveness toward Bree makes him sit her down and bow her head, and in one of the closing shots of the film she is sitting at his feet.

John Klute and Peter Cable

But the crucial placing of Klute's paternalism is in his structural relation to Cable. Diane Giddis and others have noted their close juxtaposition in the development of the narrative and the similarity of their actions in relation to Bree. Both watch her from shadows, both follow her on her assignations, Klute taps her phone, Cable tapes her sessions with her clients, both are associated visually with liftshafts, plummeting depths, screens of wire netting, shadows. Both bear towards her an intense and ambiguous staring gaze. Where the difference occurs is in their respective estimations of and judgements on the prostitute, Bree Daniels. For if the innocent Klute is something of a latter-day knightly crusader among the cesspools of contemporary decadence, and can regard the fallen Bree with a paternalist compassion, Cable, steeped in deadly experience, exhibits a distillation of the noir private eye's cynicism and moral contempt for female sexuality. The two sides of the forties private-eye stereotype's attitude to women – romantic idealisation, and embittered accusatory disgust – have been split here between two characters, representing complementary faces of patriarchy faced with the problem of female sexuality. Whereas Cable seeks to punish and destroy, representing the nineteenth-century, Victorian ethic, Klute, a modern humanitarian spirit, seeks to save. But in either case an active female sexuality, seeking sexual control for the woman's own ends, is no good, and least of all, it turns out, for the woman herself. But before we go further into what constitutes the threat of female sexuality and the contest between these two characters, it would be useful to consider the characterisation of the woman in the case.

Bree Daniels – from *femme fatale* to prostitute

The change of role in Bree Daniel's characterisation, as heroine in a thriller, from *femme fatale* to prostitute has a number of implications, and consequences. Bree Daniels has to fill the place of the film noir heroine in an investigation of female sexuality. At the same time Pakula wants to use the genre's conventions to explore issues of contemporary life. Thus the stereotype, as the centre of the film's investigative plot, must make some reference to contemporary life, must relate to more recognisable contemporary stereotypes than the rather passe *femme fatale* of 'classic' Hollywood, and must conform more closely to the needs of psychologically realistic characterisation. The ultimate effect of these modifications on the noir heroine, as I have suggested, is the relocation of woman in a place less threatening to patriarchy.

The role of prostitute as construed in this film does two things. First it has journalistic appeal as a topic recently made acceptable for public discussion and therefore can be used to evoke references to the everyday world of contemporary reality, while at the same time the idea of prostitution has the metaphoric power to refer to deeper issues of morality and personal relationships: here it represents alienated sexuality which in turn represents the alienation at the heart of our society.

As a woman, attempting to survive independently in the city, any work open to Bree Daniels depends on the marketability of the female sexual image. We first see her, totally objectified in a model line-up, where the selectors discuss the details of the female applicants' appearance as if they were so much cattle. The would-be models sit under huge mask-like empty female faces, whose features are hidden behind netted veils. Bree is next seen trying the theatre, first with a trendy director who makes it clear that bed is a condition of his helping her, then in a harshly competitive audition for the part of St. Joan. For all this, however, what *Klute* exposes in its exploration of contemporary times is not the socio-economic and related ideological structures that define women in terms of their sexual and reproductive role and create a marginal place for them within the labour market, but rather a moral, existential alienation of the psyche which is to be resolved in personal relationships, if at all.

Second, the prostitute, as an independent woman, working with other women to make a living out of men, offers a figure — especially when played by Jane Fonda, known for her supposed 'liberation' — which can accrue to itself some of the trendy modernity of the bachelor-girl stereotype and some of the more popularised aspects of the image of the liberated woman without having to stray too far from territory familiar to audience and actually broach feminism. At the same time, however, the prostitute, whose definition is based on an independent and manipulative sexuality, can fill the place of the forties noir heroine. But a reduction in the female image has taken place, for by definition the *femme fatale* is a stereotype designating the mysterious and unknowable power of women, whereas the role of prostitute represents a more defined sexual role, amenable to social control, and shorn of the earlier stereotype's fatality.

In part it is this social control that the psychotherapy sessions represent, for Bree Daniels/Jane Fonda is a special kind of prostitute, regarding her prostitution as a kind of sickness and seeking a cure. The *femme fatale* stereotype is brought further under control by the naturalisation of her temperament through psychological motivation. Bree Daniels shows many aspects of the noir heroine's temperament, approachable and loving one minute, cold and rejecting the next, but this changeability is no longer part of the grand manner of the *femme fatale*, it is simply neurotic. Her changes in mood are not incomprehensible, but motivated by a consistent psychology explained as a response to the alienating demands of modern society.

Thus some of the danger represented by the film noir heroine is mitigated by the systems of control set up in her modern counterpart's representation: *cinéma vérité* style recording of the life of a prostitute; the confessional psychotherapy sessions; psychological motivation. And in this context it is highly significant that it is largely in these psychotherapy sessions that Bree Daniels, unlike the forties *femmes fatales* who preceded her, is given an inner consciousness — the subjectivity that Diane Giddis sees as the centre of the film. I would argue, however, that it is a very circumscribed subjectivity, and in any case the power of the generic conventions accruing to the male, even in their modified form, means that a convincingly realised female subjectivity does not necessarily dominate the production of meaning in the text, and that to understand its operation in *Klute* we need to examine the relation of the psychotherapy sessions to the other investigatory structures in the film.

Woman's voice and the male gaze

So far we have not broached the question of one of the dominant devices of film noir — the voice-over. As we have already seen, the hero of *Klute*, although naming the film, is marked by his silence. On the other hand an effect of voice-over is given to the heroine, in the tapes of her conversations with her clients, and in her discourse with the psychotherapist which sometimes takes off from its image and appears over the scenes in her life which she is referring to. Thus it might seem that the woman is given power again by virtue of being given a voice. However, I would argue that it is part of the film's ideological project both to entertain the female voice and then to undermine it.

This happens in several ways. For a start, except for the deliberately mystifying introduction of her taped voice in the opening sequences of the film, Bree's voice-over is motivated and so naturalised within the narrative. Combined with the absence of flashback structure, this means her voice has little of the controlling distance often made possible in the noir use of voice-over. Then Bree's voice has been stolen from her by her aggressor, Cable, and turned against her. Words uttered in one context, are in another turned into indices of the evil which female sexuality incites in men, and are played back to her over the phone and during her final confrontation with her judge.

Thirdly the female voice that speaks of a struggle for control, for independence, for refusal of involvement and its ensuing roles of dependency and domesticity — a voice that falteringly speaks some of the themes of feminism — is undermined and contradicted by the image. This happens twice very explicitly, when Fonda's voice to the psychotherapist declares her anger at Klute's intrusion into her life and her consequent manipulation of him. What the image shows is Bree melting under the power of his gaze and touch, and subdued by her emotion, kissing his hand. Again at the end of the film her voice declares:

I know enough about myself. We're so different. Whatever lies in
store, it's not going to be setting up housekeeping in Tuscorora and
darning socks. I'd just go out of my mind . . .

— while in the image Fonda is sitting at Klute's feet. In these instances the
voice is shown to be mistaken. Bree does not know what's right for her, or
what's happening to her. Our belief in the image rather than the voice rests on
a number of factors: first, the powerful stereotype of romantic love inevitably takes precedence over these half articulations of the problems of would-
be independent women; second, the ideology of the eye and the camera as
offering first-hand evidence of reality may support the image against the
voice, and moreover Pakula's candid-camera introduction to Bree in her
opening scenes has reinforced the status of the image against whatever her
conscious voice might say to us.

  This last point raises the issue of Pakula's style in these early scenes which
establish Bree Daniels/Jane Fonda in the role of prostitute/liberated woman.
A key question is whether in these scenes she is subject or object. I would
argue that while the camera style here suggests the creation of a subject, the
character is in fact objectified. These sequences begin as social documentary,
in which Bree is the silent object in a policeman's rundown on a call-girl's life.
We then pass into a controlled candid camera observation of a typical scene
between the prostitute and her client, in which we are invited to share the
prostitute's view of events, and finally we are taken voyeuristically into the
intimacy of her home, where we are offered the spectacle of how the
bachelor-girl/prostitute spends an evening alone after her day's work.

  In the course of this progression we are encouraged to feel that we have
come closer and closer to the heroine's subjectivity, while at the same time the
moral structures of the film are being set up to leave little room for a female
point of view. So the scene between Bree and her client shows us the cool,
controlled professional on the job, but the moment when our adherence to
her point of view is clinched — when, groaning out a fake orgasm, she looks at
her watch over her client's shoulder — is also the moment which encapsulates,
however humorously, the grounds for her judgement and need of redemption.
The scene which follows closely after, in which she spends the evening at
home, continues to prepare this ground, offering, in contrast, insight into
what the 'real' woman is like. Within the conventions of candid-camera
shooting, the fact of her being alone authenticates her behaviour as natural,
unlike the role we saw her playing with her client — an authenticity reinforced by Fonda's improvisatory style of acting. We are shown details of the
bachelor-girl's attic apartment and life-style — her trendy gear, hip decor, dim
lighting, incense, dope — the conventional shorthand for the modern
'liberated' woman. At the same time the treatment of Fonda in this setting
suggests fascination with this unaccustomed image of a woman alone, an
image which evokes a certain a-sexuality in the sense that there is no man to
perform for, and which goes some way towards defining the woman as constituted for *herself*. Nevertheless this scene is also placed by the dominant
discourse which tells us what such independence 'really' means — loneliness,

insecurity, vulnerability to the male outside world, and above all, fear of men and sex.

I am not suggesting that these contradictions are not real entailments of women's struggle for independence and that the details of this scene are not sensitively observed and very recognisable, but that within the context of this film they lose their force as contradictions for female consciousness in order to be accommodated within a male fantasy of desire and fear of women. The scenes that follow, simply emphasise the vulnerability, the lost child behind Bree's mask of modernity and independence. We are shown Bree's independence at the same time as it is undermined, set up as phoney, thus preparing for the psychotherapy that follows.

But there is another structure in the film reinforcing the truth of these scenes against what the woman says, the opposition words/silence in which Klute is a pivotal figure. As I have already suggested, Klute is distinguished from his noir predecessors by his silence. But silence is also his source of power, for words are shown in this film to be deceptive, not adequate to the truth, and eventually dangerous. If Klute disdains words, he is given control within the image. The most characteristic shot of Klute is a close-up of his face, a solemn gaze assessing and ultimately controlling the scene he surveys. Within this gaze there are a number of expressions – disgust, affront, hurt, compassion – but all bearing a paternal authority. Under its power Bree gradually moves towards her redemption. Within this opposition – words/ silence: woman's voice/male gaze – the authenticity of Bree's early scenes is further reinforced. Not only is she alone, but she is silent, and although Klute's gaze is absent, she is under scrutiny of the camera and by extension the gaze of the audience.

Finally we need to consider how the psychotherapy sessions relate to the opposition of words/silence. It is significant that Bree's confessions are given to a woman, a woman who according to her profession remains also almost silent. But within the structures of this film the psychotherapist's silence has little real power. Through the series of city-life tableaux to which Bree introduces Klute, Pakula offers a critical view of urban sensibility and culture, particularly its permissive counter-culture manifestations, and the scenes with Frank Ligourin show how city life has helped to mystify Bree about her true role as a woman. Thus the need for psychotherapy is a product of the city's falseness and it is under Klute's paternal gaze that Bree unfolds.* He takes on the true priestly role – the psychotherapist merely presides, maternal, over this return of Bree to the male.

* A link between the way urban culture mystifies women about their role and the problem for patriarchy of the 'woman's voice' – her attempt to gain a position from which to speak and be heard – can perhaps be construed in Bree's choice to read for the audition the claim of St Joan to hear holy voices which she must convey to the people. Bree fails the audition, while Klute looks on.

Struggle for control over the female image

I have suggested that the dynamic of the plot of *Klute* springs from the splitting of the forties noir investigator hero into two complementary opposites who are then engaged in contest. In some ways this contest recalls the struggle in film noir between different characters for control of the story. But whereas the struggle in the forties thrillers was more often a fight to the death between hero and heroine, here the splitting of the hero means that the definition of female sexuality is contested between two male protagonists. It is now possible to flesh out this proposition. The antagonism between Klute and Cable rests in their different constructions of female sexuality which are yet two sides of the same thing. The basic threat to patriarchy which the film deals with is the possibility of women asserting their sexuality independently of men, using it to their own ends and deserting their succouring role to the male in order to gain control over him. Bree's enactment of a typical session with a 'john' demonstrates one end of the spectrum within which this threat appears; Cable's 'hell-fire' sermon at the close of the film describes the other. The scene with the 'john' shows us Bree in full sexual command of the situation, offering for payment a professional servicing of the male sexual ego. But while she offers her body and fakes orgasm, her mind is elsewhere, she is not involved. At the same time she reduces the man to a childlike dependency that is an affront to patriarchy. In this respect Klute's silent struggle for the definition of Bree is to return her to the condition of the dependent child – the natural woman, who looks lingeringly after a father carrying his child in the market, who tags happily onto Klute's coat-tails, and ends sitting at his feet, a cat in her lap, like any Gainsborough Miss.

Cable offers a more Victorian and Biblical construction on female sexuality and its ills in a rehearsal of the Edenic myth. The prostitute's attempt to control her sexuality, her claim to wield the normally male pre-rogative of words, leads her to actively engage with male sexual fantasy, instead of passively being its object. In offering the male knowledge of his own sexuality, instead of helping him maintain a veil of secrecy over it, she releases all the repression on which patriarchal civilisation is popularly based and for this she must be punished and destroyed. So Cable is able to lay the blame for all three of his murders at Bree Daniels's door; thus she comes symbolically to fill the place of the noir heroine, responsible for murder even if she has not actually sought to harm anyone. Cable's denunciation of Bree recalls Adam's excuse for eating the forbidden fruit and not a little the disappointed Victorian romantic Ruskin's outrage at the failure of women to live up to his ideals and save civilisation from the barbarity perpetrated by men:

> And whether consciously or not, you must be, in many a heart,
> enthroned: there is no putting by that crown; queens you must always
> be: queens to your lovers; queens to your husbands and your sons;
> queens of higher mystery to the world beyond, which bows itself,
> and will forever bow, before the myrtle crown and the stainless sceptre

of womanhood. But, alas! you are too often idle and careless queens, grasping at majesty in the least things, while you abdicate it in the greatest; and leaving misrule and violence to work their will among men, in defiance of the power which, holding straight in gift from the Prince of all Peace, the wicked among you betray, and the good forget. There is not a war in the world, no, nor an injustice, but you women are answerable for it; not in that you have provoked, but in that you have not hindered. Men, by their nature, are prone to fight; they will fight for any cause, or for none. It is for you to choose their cause for them, and to forbid them when there is no cause. There is no suffering, no injustice, no misery, in the earth, but the guilt of it lies with you. Men can bear the sight of it, but you should not be able to bear it. Men may tread it down without sympathy in their own struggle. but men are feeble in sympathy, and contracted in hope; it is you only who can feel the depths of pain, and conceive the way of its healing. (*Of Queen's Gardens*, p.136)[3]

The virulence of this judgement, however, is modified and assimilated to a more contemporary view of female sexuality through the reorganisation of noir narrative structure and recasting of roles. The effect of this is to redefine the woman's guilt. Male vengeance, now re-located in the criminal, is punished, but at the same time the discourse of psychotherapy that weaves through the film, together with the redefinition of the hero's role as saviour, shows the heroine's sexual philosophy to be wrong and indirectly responsible for the man's sexual crimes.

This re-location of the heroine between figures representing two sides of the noir hero is facilitated by the fact that she combines two stereotypes normally opposed in the noir thriller: victim and predator. This reorganisation of the balance of forces within the noir plot then paves the way to a rearticulation of its ending and consequent relocation of woman, and reduction of her threat by assimilation. At the beginning of the film Bree's words intrude on a family scene just as it is being destroyed through the agency of perverted sexuality. She, like any noir heroine, exists outside the family and earns an independent living from her sexuality. By the end of the film a change unprecedented in film noir has occurred in that the possibility of a fulfilled heterosexual relationship and of domesticity is posed, as Bree, despite her ironic comments about darning socks for a lifetime, goes off with Klute to the country. But by this time her *voice* has been thoroughly exposed. What we have *seen*, however, is Klute's systematic invasion of her apartment, first tidying it up, then gaining a key, and finally changing its whole style and colour scheme, from the sombre, brooding reds and purples of Bree's bachelor existence, to the cooler subdued blues and greys of domestic life. When she leaves, as some feminists have ironically noted, her room is stripped bare, but for the telephone, which no voice will answer. What Klute appears to have achieved is a rearticulation of the ending of *Double Indemnity*, arriving at the same conclusion — the heroine's realisation of the meaning of love and the return of her sexuality to its proper place – but positively rather than negatively, with less of a struggle from the woman and so with results less destructive to the male ego.

What does such a turnabout in the genre signify? In one sense the film can be seen as offering a dialogue within patriarchy between two opposing strategies in relation to the problem of female sexuality. Faced with the problem of women appearing to compete for masculine roles – here sexual assertion, the power of words, arbitration of morality, dispensation of know-ledge – the male protagonist splits, reviving a primitive type of hero, who brings a New World innocence to bear on the exhaustion of our latter-day fascistic moral guardians represented by Cable. This hero is wiser than the serpent and the woman, keeping his counsel to himself. By not committing himself to words, he doesn't run the risk of dividing against himself and so splitting and losing his identity; he retains the power of inner integrity. And in his purity he doesn't need women sexually and so is free of their power. In these respects, the hero maintains his masculine control, while appearing to take up traditionally feminine positions – silence, virginity – and eventually reconciling the wayward woman and saving her sexuality for himself. Meanwhile, Cable, the representative of the old order, is driven to self-destruction, engaging Klute in a circular investigation that leads to his own exposure and defeat. Within this structure, indicative perhaps of an ideological struggle within patriarchy to maintain control over female sexuality and its new, would-be liberating manifestations, are enmeshed fragments that refer forcefully to the images and problems of a struggling feminism.

Notes

1. Diane Giddis, op. cit.
2. *'So in Klute we don't see the countryside the detective comes from.* Exactly the opposite and quite deliberately so. At the beginning you see the missing man's family and the different society, which one won't see again. Klute carries the country with him wherever he goes. From the visual point of view, I wanted *Klute* to be a vertical film. And with Gordon Willis, the director of photography, I tried to go against the horizontal format of Panavision, by seeking out verticals. Horizontals open out, create a pastoral feeling and I wanted tension. Bree's apartment should have been seen as if at the end of a long tunnel. I framed a lot of shots with the back of another character in front, to mask a part of the screen, or made use of other sombre surfaces as masks, in order to create this feeling of claustrophobia which reflects the life of this girl [sic].', from 'Entretien avec Alan J. Pakula', op. cit., p.36.
3. John Ruskin, 'Of Queens Gardens', in *Sesame and Lilies*, George Allen and Unwin, London 1960, pp135-6.

Filmography

Angel Face
RKO 1952; *p*: Howard Hughes; *d*: Otto Preminger; *sc*: Frank Nugent and Oscar
Millard, based on a story by Chester Erskine; *ph*: Harry Stradling; *ed*: Frederick
Knudtson; *a.d.*: Albert S. D'Agostino, Carroll Clark; *m*: Dimitri Tiomkin. *l.p.*: Robert
Mitchum (*Frank Jessup*), Jean Simmons (*Diane Tremayne*), Mona Freeman (*Mary
Wilton*), Herbert Marshall (*Charles Tremayne*). 90 mins.

The Big Combo
Security-Theodora Productions 1955; *p*: Sidney Harmon; *d*: Joseph H. Lewis; *sc*:
Philip Yordan; *ph*: John Alton; *ed*: Robert Eisen; *m*: David Raksin. *l.p.*: Cornel Wilde
(*Lt. Leonard Diamond*), Richard Conte (*Mr. Brown*), Brian Donlevy (*Joe McClure*),
Jean Wallace (*Susan Lowell*), Robert Middleton (*Capt. Peterson*), Lee Van Cleef
(*Fante*). 81 mins.

The Big Heat
Columbia 1953; *p*: Robert Arthur; *d*: Fritz Lang; *sc*: Sidney Boehm, based on the
novel of the same title by William P. McGiven; *ph*: Charles Lang Jr; *ed*: Charles
Nelson, *a.d.*: Robert Peterson, *m*: Amfitheatrof. *l.p.*: Glenn Ford (*Dave Bannion*),
Gloria Grahame (*Debby Marsh*), Jocelyn Brando (*Katie Bannion*), Alexander
Scourby (*Mike Lagana*), Lee Marvin (*Vince Stone*). 90 mins.

The Blue Gardenia
Blue Gardenia Productions-Gloria Films 1953; *p*: Alex Gottlieb; *d*: Fritz Lang; *sc*:
Charles Hoffmann, based on a story by Vera Caspary; *ph*: Nicholas Musuraca; *ed*:
Edward Mann; *a.d.*: Daniel Hall; *m*: Raoul Kraushaar; 'Blue Gardenia' by Bob
Russell and Lester Lee. *l.p.*: Anne Baxter (*Norah Larkin*), Richard Conte (*Casey
Mayo*), Ann Sothern (*Crystal Carpenter*), Raymond Burr (*Harry Prebble*), Jeff
Donnell (*Sally Ellis*). 90 mins.

Build My Gallows High (see **Out Of The Past**)

Crossfire
RKO/Dore Schary 1947; *p*: Adrian Scott; *d*: Edward Dmytryk; *sc*: John Paxton; *ph*: J.
Roy Hunt; *ed*: Harry Gerstad. *l.p.*: Robert Young (*Captain Finlay*), Robert Mitchum
(*Keeley*), Robert Ryan (*Montgomery*), George Cooper (*Michell*), Gloria Grahame
(*Ginny*), Paul Kelly (*The Man*). 86 mins.

Double Indemnity
Paramount 1944; *p*: Joseph Sistrom; *d*: Billy Wilder; *sc*: Raymond Chandler and Billy
Wilder, based on the novella by James M. Cain; *ph*: John F. Seitz; *ed*: Doane
Harrison; *a.d.*: Hans Dreier and Hal Pereira; *m*: Miklos Rozsa. *l.p.*: Fred MacMurray
(*Walter Neff*), Barbara Stanwyck (*Phyllis Dietrichson*), Edward G. Robinson (*Barton
Keyes*). 107 mins.

Farewell My Lovely (US title **Murder My Sweet**)
RKO 1944; *p*: Adrian Scott; *d*: Edward Dmytryk; *sc*: John Paxton, from the novel by
Raymond Chandler; *ph*: Harry J. Wild; *ed*: Joseph Noriega; *a.d.*: Albert S.
D'Agostino; *m*: Roy Webb. *l.p.*: Dick Powell (*Philip Marlowe*), Claire Trevor (*Mrs.
Grayle*), Anne Shirley (*Ann Grayle*), Otto Kruger (*Jules Amthor*), Mike Mazurki
('*Moose' Malloy*). 95 mins.

Gilda

Columbia 1946; *p*: Virginia Van Upp; *d*: Charles Vidor; *sc*: Marion Parsonett, from the story by E. A. Ellington; *ph*: Rudolph Maté, A.S.C.; *ed*: Charles Nelson; *m*: M. W. Stoloff and Martin Skiles. *l.p.*: Rita Hayworth (*Gilda*), Glenn Ford (*Johnny*), George Macready (*Ballen*), Joseph Calleia (*Obregon*). 109 mins.

Gun Crazy

King Bros. 1949; *p*: Maurice King and Frank King; *d*: Joseph H. Lewis; *sc*: MacKinlay Kantor and Millard Kaufman, based on the *Saturday Evening Post* story by MacKinlay Kantor; *ph*: Russell Harlan; *ed*: Harry Gerstad; *m*: Victor Young. *l.p.*: Peggy Cummins (*Annie Laurie Starr*), John Dall (*Bart Tare*), Berry Kroeger (*Packett*), Morris Carnovsky (*Judge Willoughby*), Anabel Shaw (*Ruby Tare*), Harry Lewis (*Clyde Boston*), Nedrick Young (*Dave Allister*). 87 mins.

Johnny Guitar

Republic 1954; *p*: Herbert M. Yates; *d*: Nicholas Ray; *sc*: Philip Yordan, based on Roy Chanslor's novel; *ph*: Harry Stradling; *ed*: Richard L. Van Enger; *m*: Victor Young. *l.p.*: Joan Crawford (*Vienna*), Sterling Hayden (*Johnny*), Ernest Borgnine (*Bart*), Mercedes McCambridge (*Emma*). 110 mins.

The Killers

Universal 1946; *p*: Mark Hellinger; *d*: Robert Siodmak; *sc*: Anthony Veiller, based on the story by Ernest Hemingway; *ph*: Woody Bredell; *ed*: Arthur Hilton; *a.d.*: Jack Otterson and Martin Obzina; *m*: Miklos Rozsa. *l.p.*: Edmond O'Brien (*Riordan*), Ava Gardner (*Kitty Collins*), Burt Lancaster (*Swede*), Albert Dekker (*Colfax*). 105 mins.

Kiss Me Deadly

Park Lane Pictures 1955; *p*: Robert Aldrich; *d*: Robert Aldrich; *sc*: A. I. Bezzerides, based on the novel by Mickey Spillane; *ph*: Ernest Laszlo; *ed*: Michael Luciano; *a.d.*: William Glasgow; *m*: Frank Devol. *l.p.*: Ralph Meeker (*Mike Hammer*), Albert Dekker (*Dr Soberin*), Paul Stewart (*Carl Evello*). 105 mins.

Klute

Warner Bros. 1971; *p*: Alan J. Pakula; *d*: Alan J. Pakula; *sc*: Andy K. Lewis and Dave Lewis; *ph*: Gordon Willis (Panavision); *ed*: Carl Lerner; *a.d.*: George Jenkins; *m*: Michael Small. *l.p.*: Jane Fonda (*Bree Daniels*), Donald Sutherland (*John Klute*), Charles Ciotti (*Cable*), Roy Scheider (*Frank Ligourin*), Dorothy Tristan (*Arlyn Page*), Rita Gam (*Trina*), Vivian Nathan (*Psychiatrist*). 114 mins.

The Lady From Shanghai

Columbia 1948; *p*: Harry Cohn; *d*: Orson Welles; *sc*: Orson Welles, freely adapted from the novel *If I Die Before I Wake* by Sherwood King; *ph*: Charles Lawton Jr.; *ed*: Viola Lawrence; *a.d.*: Stephen Goosson and Sturges Carne; *m*: Heinz Roemheld. *l.p.*: Orson Wells (*Michael O'Hara*), Rita Hayworth (*Elsa Bannister*), Everett Sloane (*Arthur Bannister*), Glenn Anders (*George Grisby*). 86 mins.

Laura

Twentieth Century-Fox 1944; *p*: Otto Preminger; *d*: Otto Preminger; *sc*: Jay Dratler, Samuel Hoffenstein, Betty Reinhardt. Based on a novel by Vera Casparay; *ph*: Joseph La Shelle; *ed*: Louis R. Loeffler; *a.d.*: Lyle R. Wheeler and Leland Fuller; *m*: David Raksin. *l.p.*: Gene Tierney (*Laura Hunt*), Dana Andrews (*Mark McPherson*), Clifton Webb (*Waldo Lydecker*), Vincent Price (*Shelby Carpenter*). 88 mins.

The Maltese Falcon
Warner Bros. 1941; *p*: Hal B. Wallis; *d*: John Huston; *sc*: John Huston, based on the novel by Dashiell Hammett; *ph*: Arthur Edeson; *ed*: Thomas Richards; *a.d.*: Robert Haas; *m*: Adoph Deutsch. *l.p.*: Humphrey Bogart (*Sam Spade*), Mary Astor (*Brigid O'Shaughnessy*), Gladys George (*Iva Archer*), Peter Lorre (*Joel Cairo*), Sydney Greenstreet (*Casper Gutman*). 100 mins.

Mildred Pierce
Warner Bros. / First National 1945: *p*: Jerry Wald; *d*: Michael Curtiz; *sc*: Ranald MacDougall and Catherine Turney, from the novel by James M. Cain; *ph*: Ernest Haller; *ed*: David Weisbart; *a.d.*: Anton Grot; *m*: Max Steiner. *l.p.*: Joan Crawford (*Mildred Pierce*), Jack Carson (*Wally*), Zachary Scott (*Monty*), Eve Arden (*Ida*), Ann Blyth (*Veda*), Bruce Bennett (*Bert*), Lee Patrick (*Mrs. Biederhoff*). 111 mins.

Murder My Sweet (see **Farewell My Lovely**)

My Name Is Julia Ross
Columbia 1945; *p*: Wallace MacDonald; *d*: Joseph H. Lewis; *sc*: Muriel Roy Bolton, from the book *The Woman In Red* by Anthony Gilbert; *ph*: Burnett Guffey; *ed*: Henry Batista. *l.p.*: Nina Foch (*Julia Ross*), Dame May Whitty (*Mrs. Williamson Hughes*), George Macready (*Ralph Hughes*), Roland Varno (*Dennis Bruce*), Anita Bolster (*Sparkes*). 65 mins.

Night And The City
Twentieth Century-Fox 1950; *p*: Samuel G. Engel; *d*: Jules Dassin; *sc*: Jo Eisinger, based on the novel by Gerald Kersh; *ph*: Max Greene; *ed*: Sidney Stone; *a.d.*: C.P. Norman; *m*: Benjamin Frankel. *l.p.*: Richard Widmark (*Harry Fabian*), Gene Tierney (*Mary Bristol*), Googie Withers (*Helen Nosseross*), Hugh Marlowe (*Adam*), Francis L. Sullivan (*Phil Nosseross*), Herbert Lom (*Kristo*), Mike Mazurki (*The Strangler*). 101 mins.

On Dangerous Ground
RKO 1951; *p*: John Houseman; *d*: Nicholas Ray; *sc*: A.I. Bezzerides, based on his adaptation (with Nicholas Ray) of Gerald Butler's novel *Mad With Much Heart; ph*: George E. Diskant; *ed*: Roland Gross; *m*: Bernard Herrmann. *l.p.*: Ida Lupino (*Mary Madden*), Robert Ryan (*Jim Wilson*), Ward Bond (*Walter Brent*), Ed Begley (*Captain Brawley*). 81 mins.

Out Of The Past (British title **Build My Gallows High**)
RKO 1947; *p*: Warren Duff and Robert Sparks; *d*: Jacques Tourneur; *sc*: Geoffrey Homes (pseud.: Daniel Mainwaring) from his own novel; *ph*: Nicholas Musuraca; *ed*: Samuel E. Beatley; *m*: C. Bakaleinikoff. *l.p.*: Robert Mitchum (*Jeff Markham/Bailey*), Jane Greer (*Kathy*), Kirk Douglas (*Whit Sterling*), Rhonda Fleming (*Meta Carson*), Richard Webb (*Jim*), Steve Brodie (*Fisher*), Virginia Huston (*Ann Miller*). 97 mins.

Pick-up On South Street
Twentieth Century-Fox 1953; *p*: Jules Schermer; *d*: Samuel Fuller; *sc*: Samuel Fuller, from a story by Dwight Taylor; *ph*: Joe MacDonald; *ed*: Nick De Maggio; *a.d.*: Lyle Wheeler and George Patrick; *m*: Leigh Harline. *l.p.*: Richard Widmark (*Skip McCoy*), Jean Peters (*Candy*), Thelma Ritter (*Moe Williams*), Murvyn Vye (*Captain Dan Tiger*), Richard Kiley (*Joey*). 80 mins.

The Postman Always Rings Twice
MGM 1946; *p*: Carey Wilson; *d*: Tay Garnett; *sc*: Harry Ruskin and Niven Buson from the novel by James M. Cain; *ph*: Sidney Wagner; *ed*: George White; *a.d.*: Cedric Gibbons and Randall Duell; *m*: George Basserman. *l.p.*: Lana Turner (*Cora Smith*), John Garfield (*Frank Chambers*), Cecil Kellaway (*Nick Smith*), Hume Cronyn (*Arthur Keats*). 113 mins.

Scarlet Street
Diana Productions 1945; *p*: Fritz Lang; *d*: Fritz Lang; *sc*: Dudley Nichols, based on the novel and play *Le Chienne* by Georges de la Fouchardière; *ph*: Milton Krasner; *ed*: Arthur Hilton; *a.d.*: Alexander Golitzen; *m*: Hans J. Salter. *l.p.*: Edward G. Robinson (*Chris Cross*), Joan Bennett (*Kitty Marsh*), Dan Duryea (*Johnny*). 102 mins.

Sunset Boulevard
Paramount 1950; *p*: Charles Brackett; *d*: Billy Wilder; *sc*: Charles Brackett and D. M. Marshman, Jr.; *ph*: John F. Seitz; *ed*: Arthur Schmidt; *a.d.*: Hans Dreier and John Meehan; *m*: Franz Waxman. *l.p.*: Gloria Swanson (*Norma Desmond*), William Holden (*Joe Gillis*), Erich von Stroheim (*Max von Mayerling*). 111 mins.

They Live By Night
RKO 1949; *p*: John Houseman, under Dore Schary; *d*: Nicholas Ray; *sc*: Charles Schnee, based on an adaptation by Ray of Edward Anderson's novel *Thieves Like Us*; *ph*: George D. Diskant; *ed*: Sherman Todd; *m*: Leigh Harline. *l.p.*: Farley Granger (*Bowie*), Cathy O'Donnell (*Keechie*), Howard de Silva (*Chicamaw*), Jay C. Flippen (*T-Dub*). 95 mins.

Touch of Evil
Universal 1958; *p*: Albert Zugsmith; *d*: Orson Welles; *sc*: Orson Welles, freely adapted from the novel *Badge of Evil* by Whit Masterson; *ph*: Russell Metty; *ed*: Virgil W. Vogel and Aaron Stell; *a.d.*: Alexander Golitzen and Robert Clatworthy; *m*: Henry Mancini. *l.p.*: Orson Wells (*Hank Quinlan*), Charlton Heston (*Ramon 'Mike' Vargas*), Janet Leigh (*Susan Vargas*), Joseph Calleia (*Pete Menzies*). 93 mins.

Woman In The Window
Christie Corporation-International Pictures 1944; *p*: Nunnally Johnson; *d*: Fritz Lang; *sc*: Nunnally Johnson, based on the novel *Once Off Guard* by J. H. Wallis; *ph*: Milton Krasner; *ed*: Marjorie Johnson; *a.d.*: Duncan Cramer; *m*: Arthur Lang. *l.p.*: Edward G. Robinson (*Richard Wanley*), Joan Bennett (*Alice*), Raymond Massey (*District Attorney*), Dan Duryea (*Blackmailer*). 99 mins.

GUILDFORD college

Learning Resource Centre

Please return on or before the last date shown.
No further issues or renewals if any items are overdue.